Endorsements for Love, Kirsten

"Many have been touched by the tragedy of Kirsten Wolcott's murder, and now many more will be touched by this well-researched story. In these pages, the life and commitment of a student missionary unfolds with an honest look at her personal struggles and untimely death."

Gordon Bietz,
president of Southern Adventist University

"Right to the final pages that brought tears to my eyes, I couldn't put this book down. In many ways, Kirsten seemed just another college student on a short-term mission adventure. But we learn so much more—of personal struggles, spiritual growth, deep compassion. It's a story of redemption in the face of incomprehensible tragedy. Of an imperfect, but beautiful Christian young woman who loved much and was greatly loved. Of the terrible loss of a twenty-year-old martyr in running shoes."

Gary Krause,
director, Adventist Mission

"I'm so thankful for this book about my daughter. I shed tears many times. I miss Kirsten every day and can't wait to give her the longest hug when Jesus comes and my angel picks me up and takes me to her. I pray that everyone who reads this book will be changed forever."

Karen Wolcott,
mother of Kirsten Wolcott

"Kirsten's story continues to inspire students at Southern Adventist University to join the very ranks of missions in which her life was taken. This biography is honest, and creatively written. Kirsten's journal entries—skillfully woven throughout—show us her inner life, allowing Kirsten to share her story in her own words."

Brennon Kirstein,
chaplain, Southern Adventist University

Love,
Kirsten

Love,
Kirsten

Rainey H. Park
with Andy Nash

Pacific Press® Publishing Association
Nampa, Idaho
Oshawa, Ontario, Canada
www.pacificpress.com

Cover design by Steve Lanto
Photographs provided by author
Cover photo by Wyntre Robinson
Inside design by Aaron Troia

The author assumes full responsibility for the accuracy of all facts and quotations as cited in this book.

Unless otherwise noted, Scripture quotations are from The Holy Bible, English Standard Version® (ESV®), copyright © 2001 by Crossway, a publishing ministry of Good News Publishers. Used by permission. All rights reserved.

You can obtain additional copies of this book by calling toll-free 1-800-765-6955 or by visiting http://www.adventistbookcenter.com.

ISBN 13: 978-0-8163-2429-3
ISBN 10: 0-8163-2429-8

10 11 12 13 14 • 5 4 3 2 1

Table of Contents

Part 02

Foreword

When a twenty-year-old college student leaves home to be a missionary, she's supposed to be able to return home and tell stories about being a missionary. But what happens when she doesn't get to return home?

On the morning of November 19, 2009, Kirsten Wolcott was assaulted and murdered while jogging on the Micronesian island of Yap, where she volunteered as a second grade teacher. Kirsten's death shocked the Yapese people and devastated her family and friends back home in Virginia. The tragedy also left Kirsten's friends and teachers at Southern Adventist University dazed and reeling.

Several weeks later, one of Kirsten's classmates, Rainey Park, was sitting in the literary journalism class that I teach at Southern. For her course project, Rainey said she'd like to write about Kirsten Wolcott. Though Rainey didn't know Kirsten personally, she thought the story of Kirsten's life—and death—was one that needed to be told.

Over the next few months, with the gracious help of the Wolcott family, Rainey rigorously traced the final months of Kirsten's life: piecing together the events, studying Kirsten's correspondence and journal entries, and even traveling at her own expense to Yap—where she interviewed Kirsten's colleagues and the killer himself. In many ways, Rainey's passion to tell this story complements the passion that defined Kirsten's life.

Kirsten Wolcott didn't get the chance to tell her own story. So Rainey Park is telling it for her.

Andy Nash, associate professor of journalism
Southern Adventist University

Author's Note

I gathered material for this book from a number of sources. Kirsten kept a paper journal in Yap until October 20—a month before her death. She also journaled on the computer during her devotional time—jotting down notes, reflections, and prayers as she read the Bible. The last entry on her computer is from November 19, the morning she was murdered. These two sources provide a wealth of insight into Kirsten's inner and outer worlds.

In addition, I've drawn from Kirsten's e-mail during her time on Yap and interviewed dozens of people involved in this story—including Kirsten's family members, friends, fellow missionaries, and the convicted murderer.

As much as possible, I've preserved the original language of quotations, although in some cases, I've corrected spelling, grammar, or punctuation to enhance clarity for the reader. For privacy, I've changed schoolchildren's names. Also, where student missionaries' first names are similar, I've used middle names. (Kristen was changed to Liz to avoid confusion with Kirsten. Alex was changed to Gus.)

I'm particularly grateful to the Wolcott family and others who have assisted me in the telling of Kirsten's story.

Rainey H. Park
Fall 2010
www.raineypark.com

Prologue

I climb into the bed that Kirsten slept in. Across the room, in my suitcase, is Kirsten's journal: a small brown book with a suede cover and two gold-colored snaps. The last time this journal was here, on Yap, Kirsten was writing in it—filling its pages with joy and wonder, confusion and discovery.

Hey, God! It's a beautiful morning and I'm so excited for my first day in Yap . . .

My kids are great! . . .

The principal's wife chopped some young coconuts for us, put straws in them and let us drink the coconut water! Yum! It was really tasty. . . .

So today I kind of broke a rule. . . .

As much as I hate to say it, I kinda like him. . . .

I saw a lion fish and this awesome purple coral . . .

I'm down to my lowest weight in a while, but I'm not that hungry in the morning.

Solomon says there is a time for everything. As I studied, I wondered why there are both bad and good things. Why should there be a time for death?

Like you and me, Kirsten had personal struggles. She also had a contagious spirit and a vibrant faith in God. For the next two weeks, I will follow in Kirsten's footsteps, talking with her fellow student missionaries, visiting her classroom, meeting her students, and interviewing her murderer.

But first, I will rest. I close my eyes and wait for the Yapese sunrise.

PART 01

CHAPTER 01

Off and Running

Panting, Kirsten ran up the final steps wedged into the side of the mountain. From this vantage she could see the entire island stretched out below—and the clear blue Hawaiian waters glistening in the morning light.

God, You are so awesome! she thought.

Kirsten and the other island missionaries had stopped in Hawaii for three days of training. Then they would each depart for their final destination—in Kirsten's case, the tiny Micronesian island called Yap.

Final destination. Those were strange words. *I keep thinking,* she wrote in her journal, *how this isn't just a vacation. I won't be going home in a couple weeks. I'm going to be educating young kids and I don't even have an education yet. But, God, You've kept me calm and You've brought me this far. I know You won't leave me in the dark.*

God, I just have to thank You again for safety and friendship, health, nature, and all the beauty I've seen. I'm almost to my home away from home, and I can't really describe what I feel. The emotions, lack of sleep, constant change, etc., has my body confused. I'm ready to get settled in. I'm ready to get in a groove and figure out a new way of life. Use me, God, and give me extra patience, faith, hope, courage, and boldness to spread Your gospel. Prepare the hearts of those I'm coming to serve. Shine out of me and let my example show these kids and adults how amazing You really are!

Kirsten took one last look at the beautiful scenery, then ran back down to rejoin the other missionaries.

CHAPTER 02

Yap

Working at the Yap Seventh-day Adventist school wasn't Kirsten's first pick. It wasn't anyone's first pick.

No air conditioning.

No hot water.

Nowhere to go.

Yap is small—only sixteen miles long and four miles wide—much smaller than neighboring Pacific Islands.

Still, her first morning, Kirsten felt excited when she woke and took her first real look around her apartment. Cracked cream paint covered the walls. An assemblage of plaster and wooden boards held up the ceiling. The apartment wasn't much to look at, but it was surprisingly large—with three bedrooms, a kitchen, and a living area.

When the five girls arrived late the night before, Kirsten and Katherine picked the room in the farthest corner. It had a large window facing the road and the entrance to the school. There were no curtains or blinds, so when the girls woke up, Katherine tacked up a thin blanket to create a little privacy.

That afternoon the principal, Nicholas Fonseka, and his wife, Mary, took the missionaries into town. The Fonsekas were volunteers from Sri Lanka. Principal Fonseka was a stout man, with glasses and dark but graying hair. He wore linen Indian-style shirts and khaki trousers. His facial expressions were serious, and he frequently crossed his arms when he spoke—but he was known to have a good heart.

His wife, known as Miss Mary, was a petite woman, with dark hair that she wore pulled back into a ponytail. Wisps of white framed her temples. She had large, deep eyes and a smile that frequently flashed at the sight of the student missionaries.

Typically, the missionary principals only served for two years, but Principal Fonseka was now starting his third. Miss Mary would teach kindergarten.

"There's the YCA, a grocery store," Principal Fonseka said, after twenty minutes of driving. The van pulled into a small shopping plaza in the center of Colonia, the island's one and only town. A row of white buildings with small signs greeted the SMs (student missionaries) as they stepped out of the van.

Kirsten could immediately tell grocery shopping on the island would be a challenge. Inside the small gray store were several rows of shelves, mostly with canned food. Everything was imported, so the prices were high, and fresh fruits and vegetables were hard to find. Oatmeal—$7 a box. Tuna—$1.44 a can. Peanut butter—$4 for a mini-jar. Ice cream—$6 for two pints. After visiting several small stores, Kirsten found the ingredients she needed. That night she made a wonderful meal: pasta primavera with a garden medley sauce and stir-fry with peppers, onions, eggplant, and frozen broccoli. The girls offered to help Kirsten cook, but she declined.

"I really enjoy cooking," she said. "It's one of those things I have to do for my sanity—like running. I'll tell you if I ever need help."

From then on, Kirsten was the self-appointed cook.

* * * * *

Two days later, on Sunday, Kirsten was up before the sun to have worship and go for a jog. Though she had promised both her doctor and dietician that she wouldn't exercise more than three days a week on Yap, she was determined to get those three days in.

The missionaries weren't allowed to go off campus alone, so Kirsten contented herself with running around the school. First, she followed the narrow sidewalk from the apartment to the elementary playground. Then she ran around the campus, around the high school playground, and up and down the steps of the administration building. Since there wasn't much space, Kirsten made the most of her time by stopping under every covered area to do additional arm and leg exercises. All in all, her routine lasted forty minutes. Afterward she jogged back to the apartment for a cold shower—the only kind available—and breakfast.

Cereal and fresh papaya tasted soo *good after a cold shower,* she journaled. *Oh, yeah, and the bread came out great!* She had baked it the previous evening. As she ate, she thought about the other SMs.

I worry about Aila some because she hardly eats at all. I hope she doesn't lose a lot of weight. Been there and done that and now it scares me!

* * * * *

Kirsten's job assignment on Yap was teaching second-graders. Since the kids already spoke English, she would teach them a variety of subjects, much like second grade back home. As she prepared her classroom—scrubbing desks, taking down the prior year's decoration, writing lesson plans—Kirsten thought about the year to come.

God, I want more than my accent, my skin, and my clothes to tell me apart while I'm here on Yap, she prayed. *I want to be firm in what I believe. Help me not to be a drifter anymore. I want to know what I believe and live it. Give me the strength to be bold! When we have issues I know that YOU are the only One who can get me out. Sure, I have my principal and coordinators, but when it comes down to You, You are the One that is mighty to save! Come be my strong tower in my life. Fill me with the power of Your Spirit and give me the will to be able to serve You faithfully today. I want to shine for You and make someone's day brighter.*

* * * * *

When school started two weeks later, Kirsten felt nervous. She wished that she'd had a chance to talk with her mom the night before—but the Internet was down. She woke up at 5:30 A.M., grabbed her flashlight, and went for a run—down the sidewalk, around the campus, around the high school playground, and up and down the steps of the administration building. By 7:00 A.M., she was in her classroom, ready to meet and greet her new students. There were ten of them—a *perfect* ten: three boys and seven girls. Each was dressed in the school uniform of maroon shorts or a skirt and a cream colored shirt. As they came in, the students left their shoes at the door.

The first lessons were difficult. Kirsten tried to introduce the subjects slowly, but by the afternoon the kids seemed worn out. The only activity that caught their interest was looking at maps and learning about other countries.

Help! she journaled that evening. *OK, God, here's the long and short . . . my kids are great! So cute, listen pretty well, but are not up to speed as far as learning goes. I have some that can barely read, others who can't add or subtract; they can't count by twos, they don't know how much a dime is worth. They really try (most of them), but it's tough. . . . They are quite needy right now and seem to ask permission about everything, which is good in some cases, but bad in others!*

They do work very quietly and well when they have a task to do. I really appreciate that. . . . I hope that everything goes smoothly from here on out. . . . Please give me some peace so I can calm myself and sleep tonight. Thanks, God. Amen. Ke

In addition to the challenge of teaching, Kirsten felt the stress of larger school issues. *Principal told us today that the school is having some troubles,* she journaled. *We have no teachers for English or Bible (high school). The couple that was coming doesn't want to come unless they get paid, but we can't afford that! And some of the others are having trouble with their papers and such!*

The school had no secretary, treasurer, maintenance and grounds crew, or any other administrators. The Fonsekas did it all. To help balance their responsibilities, they appointed Katherine vice principal of the high school. Kirsten prayed that things would improve, and she resolved to keep a good attitude.

God, she wrote, *I know that the devil is working hard to bring this school down and make it so we get discouraged or frustrated, but we need some extra faith. Thanks that You've promised never to leave us or forsake us, and that You've promised You would supply all our needs according to Your riches in glory. . . .*

Paul promises that when we stand strong in the Lord, our life can be full. We all need to encourage each other and help build each other's faith. God, I'm so thankful for my group of girls. Help me to be an encouragement to someone today. Use me to brighten their day. God, I just feel like my faith isn't as strong as it should be. . . . I want to trust You because I know You love this school and can take care of it, and You will. I believe that You can do amazing things for us here, but God, there is still that twinge that stresses me out, the one that thinks I CAN'T live without a copy machine. So just like those in the Bible, help my unbelief.

Bring us teachers and the other resources that we need to grow and be a good witness for You. Please help my love to grow more and more for the kids, this place, and the people here. I want to love others with the special kind of love so I can reach them. . . . Thanks so much for Your love and how You died so that I can be forgiven and free. I'm thankful for the freedom and that assurance. I'm also really thankful that I can talk to You every morning and lay all my random stresses and burdens and random thoughts on You. Again, I ask for Your special strength this morning. Guide me so that I can live for You. Grant me Your special peace. Thanks, God, for Your love. Help me to share it. Talk to Ya later. Ke

* * * * *

After a hard first week of school, Kirsten was looking forward to some Sabbath rest. She and the other missionaries enjoyed waking up later than usual on Saturday morning before piling into the van and driving the twenty-five minutes to the local Adventist church.

The white building was small, with rows of flowers and tropical plants out front. Inside, the tile floors felt cool on Kirsten's bare feet. Ceiling fans whirred silently above, while a cross-breeze moved in through the large windows.

Officially, there were about sixty Adventist members on the island, but fewer than thirty showed up each week. The SMs quickly learned that if they ever saw the letters TBA—To Be Announced—in the bulletin, one or more of them would be called on to play the piano, deliver the sermon, teach Sabbath School, or sing special music.

I like having things to do, Kirsten journaled, *but it also gets tiring.*

CHAPTER 03

Breaking a Rule

Nothing rejuvenated Kirsten like jogging. She was delighted when Katherine agreed to run with her on some days, because that meant the two could venture off campus.

"I haven't jogged for a while," Katherine said their first morning. "But I'd like to get back into it."

As Katherine puffed up the hills, she noticed how easily Kirsten ran and talked at the same time.

"You have to use the hills to your advantage," Kirsten said, slowing her pace to match Katherine's. She explained a technique a running mentor had taught her: smaller steps on the way up, longer ones on the way down. As they ran, the two young women chatted about school, family, religion, and tastes.

"How come you always walk around on tiptoe?" Katherine asked.

Unlike most people, Kirsten strode from toe-to-heel, like she was prancing—walking on air somehow. Even when she cooked or taught, it wasn't uncommon for her to stand on tiptoe.

"I can't help it," Kirsten laughed. "This is how I've always walked, ever since I was little. When I tried to learn how to walk from heel-to-toe, it was really hard. My muscles weren't used to stretching that way and it hurt. It's more comfortable for me to run and walk like this."

It took the girls fewer than fifteen minutes to run to Tom's Store and back. Though it was a short jaunt, Kirsten enjoyed every step of it. It was freeing to have a long, straight stretch where she could run at full speed rather than jumping over potholes or darting around corners.

Kirsten's love for exercise found another outlet in biking. She and another student missionary, Liz, decided to buy bikes on one of their Thursday town trips.

"Can we ride them back to school?" the girls asked Principal Fonseka, as he dropped them off at the hardware store. He consented.

In front of the hardware store was a modest rack of bikes.

"Guess there's not much selection here," Liz said, pulling out a bike the color of Mountain Dew. "This looks like a twelve-year-old's bike!"

Kirsten picked out her own. It was purple and silver, with the number 26 painted near the front. The girls paid for the bikes and started back to the school.

A cool breeze accompanied them as they rounded the curve and rode along the shore. It carried a mixture of sweet and rancid scents. For five minutes, the girls enjoyed the bliss of easy bike riding. Then they came to a hill. Kirsten zoomed to the top and looped back before Liz made it up the first time.

"I don't know how many more of these hills I can take!" Liz panted several hills later. "I think I'm going to throw up."

Kirsten thought, *Maybe it's that granola bar and peach nectar you had.*

"I think I'll just walk up the hills," Liz said, dismounting.

A few mornings later, Kirsten convinced Liz to wake up early and go for a moonlight ride. The dogs greeted them as they padded down the stairs and walked around to the back of the apartment building. They unlocked the storage closet and pulled out their bikes, then fastened their headlamps and set out in the dark.

The air was cool and calm, and at 5:30 A.M., they had the road to themselves. They pedaled for fifteen minutes—past Tom's Store, past Yap's Grand Canyon, past the bar on the left—up and down the hills and slopes, around the curves, until they came to a gravel road.

"We should probably turn around," Kirsten said.

"Yeah," Liz agreed.

They looped back toward the school. By now the sun was coming up behind them—hot pink and orange streaks lighting up the sky. The ride was exhilarating, but for Kirsten it wasn't enough; her muscles and body were just waking up. After breakfast, worship, and showering, Kirsten went to her classroom early and did an ab workout on the alphabet mat.

* * * * *

It wasn't long before Kirsten realized that neither Katherine nor Liz enjoyed exercising as much as she did.

"Can I bike alone if I'm careful?" she asked Principal Fonseka one afternoon. He agreed.

Kirsten pranced to the storage closet, retrieved her bike, and hit the road. It was so liberating just to ride! Climbing the hills, she could feel the muscles tensing in her legs—and she loved every minute of it. Going down was a second reward. The wind whipped her face, cooling her skin, and blowing her stray curls away. She rode almost all the way to the beach. To feel this freedom every day would be amazing. The only thing better than biking . . . would be running!

The next morning was overcast and rainy. Katherine had said she would run with Kirsten, but changed her mind when she saw the downpour. Kirsten waited inside, having devotions and praying for the rain to stop.

Morning, God. It's so weird. Every night it's been raining. I'm not really sure why but it has. I like it 'cause it cools things down, but

I also pray that You help it stop so that Katherine and I can go run-ning. It's really tough if I have to run later! I really feel like I need to run. I had a bad night last night. First, someone came around and squealed their tires and it scared me so bad and woke me up. Then someone pulled into the driveway and the dogs were going crazy (right outside our window of course). God, You know that I really need that "pick me up" in the morning.

The rain persisted. Kirsten waited. Finally, she left.

Later that day she journaled: *Hey God, so today I kinda broke a rule. I went jogging (in the rain!) down the road by* myself! *I just didn't feel like the same old thing and running through wet grass and puddles and the like. It felt so great to just go! I mean, wow! It was very invigorating even though it was all wet.*

CHAPTER 04

"Please, Keep Me Safe"

As the school year progressed, Kirsten felt like she was getting into the hang of things. *I feel like a super mom*, she journaled. *Get up early to jog, eat, shower, teach school, review for the next day, make dinner for my crew, and then prepare more for the next day. I like it, though! It keeps me busy and it's doing things I like to do.*

With time she'd gotten a better feel for the abilities of her students, and her relationship with God was growing. That Sabbath she flipped open her Bible and read from 2 Timothy 2.

> You then, my child, be strengthened by the grace that is in Christ Jesus, and what you have heard from me in the presence of many witnesses entrust to faithful men who will be able to teach others also. Share in suffering as a good soldier of Christ Jesus. No soldier gets entangled in civilian pursuits, since his aim is to please the one who enlisted him. An athlete is not crowned unless he competes according to the rules. It is the hard-working farmer who ought to have the first share of the crops. Think over what I say, for the Lord will give you understanding in everything.
>
> Remember Jesus Christ, risen from the dead, the offspring

of David, as preached in my gospel, for which I am suffering, bound with chains as a criminal. But the word of God is not bound! Therefore I endure everything for the sake of the elect, that they also may obtain the salvation that is in Christ Jesus with eternal glory. The saying is trustworthy, for:

> If we have died with him, we will also live with him; if we endure, we will also reign with him; if we deny him, he also will deny us; if we are faithless, he remains faithful—for he cannot deny himself (verses 1–13).

Kirsten let the words sink in. *It's so amazing to me how God can use anyone and all we need to do is share. Please give me the boldness and courage to share, especially when the evangelistic meetings are coming up.*

God, I want to be like a good soldier, faithful and brave, fighting only for my Commander. I also want to be like an athlete who is fast and determined, who can pace themselves and follow all the rules to win the prize. They have to train and work at it to improve, and they are always seeking to get a better time and to improve themselves. I want to be like a farmer who is hearty and strong. They work long hours and tirelessly and patiently wait for their reward. I think it's cool how Paul uses all these examples to meet people where they were so that they could relate to the different jobs for that time. God, Paul was so neat.

She finished reading the chapter, focusing on Paul's warning not to quarrel about words and to avoid useless talk.

We need to be careful, as workers for God, how we act. We shouldn't argue about certain wording because that never helps anyone and it actually may HURT those who are listening and who don't know the whole story, or don't have the spiritual knowledge that we have. We should try and make our lives acceptable to Jesus.

Of course He takes us where we are, but that doesn't mean that we should ever say, "Oh, this is good enough!" NO! We should always strive for more! God, I want to be a strong worker—one who is not ashamed and who can teach what is right and true!

Help me to stay away from foolish and useless talk. I feel like we mostly do that here but back home there are times when our conversations are far from what they should be! God, today I want You to use me. I want to be like those gold and silver things that are used for special purposes, but I also want to be the wood and clay things that are used for the everyday ordinary jobs! I just want to be useful to You, ready to do ANY work that is good and that You want me to do. That's a little scary, but I know that with Your help, I can do anything! I want to run away from evil and work to live right and how You would want me to. Help me to have faith, love, and peace, and give me a pure heart.

God, I don't want to be involved with foolish arguments or quarreling because that's just not worth it! I want to be kind to everyone, a good teacher, and patient! Oh God, that's one of my biggest goals especially while I'm here on Yap! You know I can't believe I'm teaching! I can't believe I'm doing what I'll be doing for the rest of my life! This is my job and this is what I'll be doing! Yet, I still have to go back and finish two years of school. I'm excited to become a BETTER teacher in some ways and in others, I just want to keep going. I want to see what it's like to teach in America, to teach where the kids (or at least most of them) are on level. Wow, that would be so different, so enjoyable. Yet God, my class is so amazing and I'm so thankful for each one of them! They really aren't hard to manage at all! Help me to be gentle, yet firm, and share You with them and also help them learn! Grow me and help me to be willing to accept constructive criticism! Thanks again for the Sabbath rest and the weekend as a whole! Love You, Amen!

* * * * *

No sooner had Kirsten thanked the Lord for a manageable class than things became challenging. On Monday morning, a new boy arrived without warning and joined the second grade. He was from one of the outer islands and barely spoke any English. Questions flurried through Kirsten's brain. *Where will he sit? What about my perfect ten? How can I catch him up?* His presence completely threw her off.

Kirsten also received news that several other students would be leaving since their families were moving to another island. *Too many changes for one child's brain—mine!* she told God.

* * * * *

Kirsten became so occupied with work that for several days she didn't have time for her morning runs. Finally, on Wednesday afternoon, she had a short break and again asked the principal if she could ride alone—since Liz's bike was broken. This time he said No.

ARRG! Kirsten thought. She needed the exercise to help her decompress. Without it, she felt horrible.

Thursday morning brought clear skies, and nothing was going to get in the way of her jog. *Please keep me safe as I run,* she prayed. *God, help the board members to allow us to run or bike by ourselves! Oh, it's so annoying! I know it's for our safety but . . . I dunno.*

As her feet pounded the pavement, Kirsten reflected on the events of the week. One of her students told her about her uncle coming home drunk and having a fight with her dad. At night the student couldn't sleep because she kept seeing the image of her relatives fighting. It weighed heavy on Kirsten's heart.

Poor thing! she thought. *My kids know too much about alcohol and being drunk. Please be with them and help them to be safe!*

Her mind wandered to the entire class. *You know I don't have culture-shock and I'm not really homesick, but I realized how depen-*

dent I am on my kids. If they have a good day, are happy, understand a lesson, whew! *It makes my day! But if I tried so hard and they still don't get it, man, I feel so depressed and sad, and it just brings me down.*

Fortunately, there were some things to celebrate. Kirsten's class had earned twenty good points on her reward and discipline chart and she was going to throw a party for them next Friday. Also, things were going better than expected with the new student. He was good at math and liked to sing. That gave Kirsten something to work with.

Thanks so much for this great teaching opportunity and fun time that I can have here on Yap. It really is a beautiful place. I'm so glad that You love me with an everlasting love. Help me to please You today. I'm happy to be Your child today. Fill my heart, mouth, and body with You . . . Love You. Ke

CHAPTER 05

Changes

In mid-September a batch of new missionaries arrived. Ana was the first. She loved running, but unlike Kirsten, preferred evenings over mornings.

Despite the rule about not leaving campus unaccompanied, Ana frequently jogged alone. The principal tried to put a stop to it, but no amount of talking seemed to restrain her.

One afternoon the two crossed paths, and the principal confronted her again.

"Remember that you're not allowed to run alone off campus," the principal said.

"Why not?" she asked. "I'm twenty-seven years old. I am old enough to take responsibility for myself."

"It's not up to me," he said. "It's the decision of the school. If you want to talk to the board members and tell them how you feel, maybe you can ask them at the upcoming meeting if you can go by yourself."

Ana agreed.

A few days after Ana's arrival, two more missionaries landed on Yap. Kirsten couldn't run with Sterling or Alex because guys and girls weren't allowed to spend time one-on-one. Nevertheless, their arrival was exciting news. In addition to filling a desperate need for teachers, Sterling and Alex added a fun dynamic to the group. The two had known each other since elementary school and played perfectly into each other's antics and jokes.

They add a certain goofiness to everything, Kirsten journaled. *As much as I hate to say it, I kinda like him.*

"Him" was Sterling—the prototypical tall, dark, and handsome. He had a studied casualness that showed whenever he flashed a smile and brushed a renegade strand of wavy black hair out of his face. But it wasn't just his looks that caught Kirsten's attention.

He's really funny, musical, and an all around good spiritual guy who likes to have fun! Kirsten wrote. *Nothing will become of it, but I can't stop random thoughts.*

* * * * *

Now that all the teachers had arrived, a special meeting was called to familiarize them with the local customs and rules. The missionaries met in the chapel, where the pastor's wife had prepared a special lunch. Principal Fonseka began by reading out of the handbook and expounding on the points. *Don't leave a female student alone with a male student. Don't fraternize with student missionaries of the other gender. Don't go off campus alone.*

"Any questions?" he asked when he was finished.

Ana wanted to bring up the issue of exercising alone off campus, but before she could, Alex raised his hand.

"A lot of times my fourth grade girls give me a hug before or after class," he said. "Does that violate any of the rules?"

"It's OK," the principal said. "Any other questions?"

Again, Ana raised her hand, but someone else was called on first. Ana tried to be patient while the principal answered the question, but she felt an increasing need to use the restroom. She decided to slip out and ask the question when she got back. But in her absence, the principal brought up the subject.

"Some of you have asked me about running alone off campus,"

he said. "We will discuss it now in front of the board members."

"Why is that rule in place?" someone asked.

"Several years ago," the principal said, "there was a girl who was raped."

"That's not the only instance," another board member said. "Not long ago a pastor and his family were murdered in Palau. This area can seem very safe, but you never know. Of course, we can't force anyone to stay on campus, but we're legally responsible for you, so we wouldn't want anything to happen."

By this time Ana had returned.

"What if," she said, "we get some sort of permission from our parents, or write one ourselves saying we take responsibility for whatever happens?"

The board members launched into discussion.

"I think it would be OK," one said. Another strongly disagreed.

The SMs watched as they argued back and forth. Finally, they came to an agreement: if you get a letter of permission from your parents, you can run alone off campus.

"Can that apply to biking as well?" Kirsten asked.

"Yes," the principal answered. "It will apply to exercising in general."

That night Kirsten excitedly wrote home.

Hey Mom,

The school board said we can now exercise alone if we write up a thing basically saying that they aren't responsible if anything happens and they get an e-mail from our parents OKing it. So could you send me an e-mail saying that you give me permission to exercise alone! PLEASE!!! I'll be super careful and only do it when absolutely necessary!

Love you bunches!

XOXO,

Ke

* * * * *

That weekend Kirsten used an Internet phone to call her mom. Sometimes she talked with her dad as well, but often he would just jot down questions for Karen, Kirsten's mom, to ask, and she would fill him in on the answers later. This week he wanted to know more about the exercise issue.

"Your dad was wondering why the school board changed the rule," Karen said. "We trust the administration to know what's safest, but it seems kind of odd that they would change the rules this far into the school year."

Kirsten did her best to explain the situation to her mom, but then decided to e-mail her dad directly, addressing his specific questions and concerns.

Hey Dad,

The reason I have to exercise alone is because no one will exercise with me on most days. On the days when I can get someone to exercise with me, I do it with them. SO, I can only exercise on the campus and that's *sooo* boring after a while!

If you want me to only exercise alone when it is daylight hours, that's fine. And if you want me to just stay on the main roads, I can. But in the morning no one is even out. I don't usually see any cars until around 6:00 or later. I don't have mace because I couldn't take it on the airplane with me. I don't think it's illegal. LOL! There aren't really many rules here! There aren't blocks! Hehe, so yes, I'll be going some miles from the school.

. . . No one gets up early. One of the other girls likes to run, but she won't run early in the morning. There really aren't many runners. I see some people biking. OK, pretty much you don't understand this type of place. People don't just run or bike or do anything just for fun (well, maybe drink). Everything is about survival and working.

Um, there's a sports complex that's kinda close but I haven't been there yet so I don't know what's there. I know there's a track and tennis courts, but that's all I know for sure.

OK, jump rope, um sure. Can we say BORING! I think I'd rather run around the complex. At least there's a change of scenery. Besides, I don't have a jump rope!

Oh my, I never exercise with music unless I'm inside, even in the States. It's too dangerous, besides I like to think/pray/sing/etc., to myself. And if it makes you feel any better, sometimes the dog goes with me. So I guess for now I'll keep going on the complex, blah, and hope that maybe Katherine will go with me!

XOXO,
Ke

Kirsten was frustrated about her parents' deliberation, but hoped her answers would cause her dad to reconsider.

* * * * *

The next e-mail Kirsten received from her dad was disappointing to say the least.

Hi Peep,
Sorry to hear such a martyr tone to the letter. Remember this is your dad, and I am on your side. I guess the best I can do is to tell you the story your mormor told me about when she was 16–20—somewhere in that age range—and the German soldiers invaded her town. She was so excited and curious about all the goings-on that she just HAD to go to the town square and watch. Her mom told her absolutely

NOT, and she argued so hard that she was going that her mom finally could not get across to her the danger involved and finally slapped her across the face to get some sense into her head. The only time in her life her mom ever slapped her. Now of course she says, "I was so foolish and bullheaded, I had no idea of the danger and just wouldn't listen."

At this point the only definite thing that I can see you are having a problem with is boredom, so suck it up and use some common sense. If lots of islanders were jogging and biking, then joining in with them would be fine. If they don't and you do, then you just marked yourself with a big X. Try to be creative and work within safety boundaries. You won't believe the cool things you can do with a jump rope if you practice a little. Plus you can teach it at least to your girl students.

Dad

Kirsten couldn't believe it. Her parents were being ridiculous! Hastily, she typed back a response.

COME ON!! YOU GUYS ARE KILLING ME!!! So I can't even BIKE by myself? I bought this bike and now I can't even use it! This is totally crazy!

Without adding another word, she hit Send.

CHAPTER 06

Disordered Eating

Next to running, cooking was one of Kirsten's favorite things to do. She had hundreds of recipes stored on her computer, and she liked the challenge of having to make do with the ingredients on Yap. To supplement the lack of fruits and vegetables, she planted a garden in her classroom and scoured the campus looking for taro, papayas, coconuts, and mangoes. Whenever Kirsten couldn't find all the ingredients she needed for a particular recipe, she'd "Yapify" the meals—substituting a called-for item with one of her local finds.

Kirsten was also great at whittling recipes down. Once Olivia baked vegan chocolate cupcakes. Kirsten grabbed one and walked into her room.

"Have you tried Olivia's vegan chocolate cupcakes?" Kirsten asked Katherine, who was seated on the bed. "They are *sooo* good, but I want to try to modify the recipe so it will be healthier and have fewer calories."

"How many calories are in the original cupcake?" Katherine asked.

"*Mmm* . . . about two hundred to two hundred and fifty per cupcake," Kirsten said as she pulled out her computer and opened a blank document.

"Let's see," she wondered aloud. "What could I substitute to cut down on the calories?"

She thought for a few moments, then had an epiphany. "Applesauce! I could use applesauce instead of oil, and that could count for the liquid as well, so I could cut that out. And I could use coconut milk to replace something else . . ."

After a few more clicks, Kirsten had produced a modified recipe. The new cupcakes only contained 98 calories.

* * * * *

While Kirsten continued cooking for the girls upstairs, they rarely, if ever, shared a meal with the guys. One day in late September, Kirsten suggested that the guys and girls take turns cooking a Friday evening meal for the entire group. Everyone agreed, and Kirsten quickly organized a menu for the first weekend. She took the lead in making a Mexican black bean soup and homemade bread, while the others pulled the large dining room table from the girls' apartment onto the porch.

The dinner was delicious. Kirsten didn't eat much herself, but she liked spending time with the group. Conversation ranged from childhood stories to memorable classroom moments.

"I remember how for the longest time I couldn't understand why none of my students would answer my questions," Aila said. "Then finally someone told me that in Yapese culture people raise their eyebrows several times to say Yes."

Everyone laughed. They resonated with Aila's initial confusion.

Kirsten spoke up. "When I gave my first real spelling and science tests," she said, "most of my kids did pretty well, but a few had obviously never taken a test before. It was funny because they just circled everything! I explained to them that they only needed to circle one—the right answer. It was so cool to see how much they've improved from the pre-test to the post-test."

"Once," Olivia said, "I did a class demonstration and showed the students a cell with one of the microscopes. They thought it was so cool that they wanted to look at something else, so one student said, 'Let's look at some lice under the microscope!' And then this other boy was like, 'Ooh, Ben has lice!' So they proceeded to pick a louse from their friend's head. I was so disgusted! I kept saying, 'No, no! Put it back!' But they squashed it and smeared it on their papers."

"Oh, my goodness," Katherine said. "Are lice that common that it's no big deal to them? I hope I don't get lice!"

Kirsten enjoyed sharing with the SMs. *Each is unique and has something to offer,* she thought. *A good mix, I think. Seems like we've known each other forever.*

Someone's question interrupted her thoughts. "Aren't you going to eat anything?"

"Oh, I'm not very hungry," Kirsten answered. "I snacked while I cooked."

* * * * *

This wasn't the first time someone had commented on Kirsten's eating habits. Two years earlier, Kirsten's freshman year of college, her roommate, Wyntre, started asking questions. Wyntre noticed that Kirsten measured everything and counted all her calories. For breakfast she ate a half serving of cereal and several fruits. Lunch was often a serving of Brussels sprouts and a small bowl of dressingless salad. Dinner was a baked potato and trail mix. Though Kirsten said she was just trying to eat healthfully, her concern with food sometimes seemed excessive.

"Don't you think you're maybe getting too skinny?" Wyntre asked.

"I like how I look," Kirsten replied.

The conversation ended there, but Wyntre kept watch.

After months of noticing Kirsten's increased physical activity and dwindling food intake, Wyntre finally confronted Kirsten. They were eating together in the cafeteria when Kirsten leaned over to slip a few books in her backpack.

"Oh, my goodness," Wyntre said. "I can see your entire backbone through your sweatshirt."

Kirsten sat up. Usually she brushed such comments off, but this time her face registered a small amount of worry.

"Listen," Wyntre said, "either you call your mom, or I will."

"I'll call," Kirsten said.

* * * * *

Later that week Karen Wolcott answered her phone.

"Mom," Kirsten said, "I need to talk to you. I think I'm too skinny."

"Are you eating enough?" Karen asked.

"Not really."

"Well, why not?"

"I can't," she said.

"What do you mean you can't?" Karen said, worry in her voice. She remembered Kirsten looking a little slimmer than usual the last time she saw her, but she thought that was the normal result of college stress and exercise. Was something else wrong?

Kirsten didn't answer. She didn't know how.

"Well, you could just eat," Karen said. "There's food. We have money. We're not destitute. You don't have to be on starvation rations."

"No, I can't," Kirsten said.

Silence.

"Well," Karen finally said, "I'll call the doctor and see what we need to do."

"OK," Kirsten said.

Long after Karen hung up, the conversation ran through her mind. She shared it with Hollis, Kirsten's father.

"Food is food," he said. "What's the big deal?"

* * * * *

"Some people have eating disorders," Elisabeth said. "Others just have disordered eating."

Kirsten was at her first appointment with Elisabeth Peterson, a dietician who was going to help Kirsten work out her feelings about food and learn to eat a more balanced diet. Prior to the appointment, Kirsten filled out a sheet about her medical and family history, weight, and social behaviors.

Kirsten wrote that she jogged forty to fifty minutes three days a week. In addition, she often biked, walked, and did calisthenics. Her consciousness with food had begun as an innocent attempt to be healthier at the age of seventeen. Somewhere along the way, things got out of balance, and Kirsten was now only consuming as many calories as she burned exercising.

Elisabeth read the sheet and addressed Kirsten. "The place to start is with understanding your body's needs. The body is a bio-chemical machine. Just like any other machine, it requires fuel and specific tools to do the job of sustaining life, facilitating growth, maintaining repairs, and fighting diseases. We're going to focus on working in nutrients that will heal your body and give you more energy. We want you to be in a healthy place with your weight so you can live the type of lifestyle you would like."

Kirsten was eager to learn. Together she and Elisabeth formed a meal plan that included the right amounts of nutrients and proteins.

"I want you to follow this for a while," Elisabeth said. "And then once we get your body well nourished, we'll start moving towards intuitive eating."

"What's that?" Kirsten asked.

"It's when you eat based on your body's cues—eat when you're hungry, stop when you're full—rather than based on a time of day or what someone says you should be eating. We were all born intuitive eaters, but many people get disconnected from themselves. My goal is to help you reconnect with your normal eating cues."

Elisabeth knew it would be scary for Kirsten to start adding calories to her diet, but following the meal plan usually gave her clients a sense of security and control until they could learn to trust her.

"First we have to heal your body; then we can start working with your mind."

* * * * *

For the next several sessions, Elisabeth tracked Kirsten's progress, worked with her on new skills, and began analyzing Kirsten's feelings about food.

"Remember that when you feel like restricting, it's not about the food. Food is the lightbulb reminding you to check in with your feelings and needs. It's really about what's going on underneath.

"Eating disorders serve a purpose. It could be coping with a stressful situation, or with feeling hurt or overwhelmed. Or you might be suppressing an uncomfortable feeling such as shame, loneliness, or a traumatic experience that causes you to feel powerless. When you're not able to identify those feelings and use healthy coping skills to manage them, you may feel tempted to turn to controlling food, just like others turn to drugs and alcohol."

Kirsten realized the root of her problem was twofold.

[I was] always looking at my body and not really thinking I was fat, she journaled. *But not really being completely happy, satisfied,*

or comfortable with my body. The other part was a need for some control, because things were more stressful and I needed to handle them and keep things straight. . . .

Stress is one of the things that makes me restrict. It's when I feel like everything else in my life is out of control and I'm just being pushed along with life, that I feel most powerful by controlling what I eat. It makes me feel strong to think that I only ate 200 calories for breakfast. It makes me feel like I can do anything, and I can deal with anything. I don't really understand why or how I got to that point, but I'm there and it's a constant struggle.

* * * * *

By the end of the summer, Kirsten had made a lot of progress, but Elisabeth wasn't ready to let go of her yet. She knew eating disorders can take anywhere from two to ten years to heal, so when Kirsten returned to Southern for her sophomore year, Elisabeth made sure they had periodic phone conversations. Kirsten also went to the university health center once a week to be weighed, and the results were faxed to Elisabeth.

In the meantime, Kirsten continued to process her feelings about food. Elisabeth had once said that a relationship with food could be a lot like a bad relationship with a boyfriend. "Sometimes," she said, "it's helpful to name our problem with food so that we can realize it's something separate from ourselves and learn how to divorce ourselves from it."

Kirsten decided to name her eating disorder Kayn.

As Kayn grows and becomes a full grown man, he has become my abusive boyfriend, she journaled. *I love him even though he hurts me, and I just can't let him go. Sometimes I get up my courage and ask for help and I leave him for a while, but he always somehow slips back in my head and I end up running back to him. Eventually, he will bring death, but for now he looks and feels good. . . .*

I want to get better and I know what my body needs, but my body is weak. I can't make myself do it. That old relationship is strong and controlling. I give in to my mental struggle and run back to my old relationship because it's comfortable there, and it's powerful there. It feels good there and it makes me feel good. . . .

Kirsten prayed every day for God to help her overcome her eating disorder, but a part of her didn't want to give it up. *I love it and it loves me,* she journaled. *It gives me power and makes me feel strong and in control. I want to get better, I want to be normal, but yet in some morbid way, I'm just not ready to let go of my relationship with Kayn . . .*

Over time, Kirsten began to feel that exercise, food, and image were becoming idols to her.

While anorexia isn't an actual material, physical thing, it's still something that I'm worshiping because, honestly, I spend more time thinking about what I'm going to eat or looking up how many calories are in something than I spend in my morning devotions. I thought to myself, "What if every time I had a question about God or something spiritual, I search as diligently as I do to find out calorie contents of different things?" That thought crushed me. I felt like I had let God down because I really wasn't putting Him first. I have let these thoughts control me instead of letting His will control my life.

Kayn feels good, but is really doing harm. So long, Kayn, I'm officially breaking up with you! I've found Someone better, Someone who will take my issues because He actually cares for me. He will never pull me down into sin, but will always lift me up as His child. I never want to see you again, Kayn, so get out of my life. You no longer have the right to mess with me or touch me because this relationship is over! God, I commit my body to You.

My prayer is that God can use me even with my sickness and my abusive "boyfriend" to reach people. I'm not perfect and I'm STILL struggling, but in the meantime, God, give me courage to use this sickness for You.

When Kirsten left for Yap, she had made even more improvement, but she still had to watch her weight and limit her exercise.

"It's natural for this to be triggered during transitions or in a new environment," Elisabeth said. "Since it's an old coping skill, you may be tempted to fall back on it in stressful situations, but now you know how to recognize it and move forward."

Kirsten tried to take those words to heart.

CHAPTER 07

Permission Letter

In late September, the swine flu hit Yap. As a precautionary measure, classes were canceled for three weeks. By the first morning of the break, Kirsten could already sense how difficult it was going to be to fill her time.

God, I ask that You help me take just one day at a time, she prayed. *I know that there's not a lot I can do except take it slow and do my thing. Please let me take this time to do good for You. God, if it's Your will please help it not to last that long. God, I really don't want to miss three weeks of school. My kids really need to be in school, and I really need them! Show me what it is You want me to do.*

Reluctantly, she dressed and went to work in her classroom: cleaning, sorting, and rearranging things.

Kirsten still hadn't received a reply from her dad, so that evening she decided to use some of her extra time to write him another e-mail.

> Dad,
>
> I talked to some of the other girls that teach HS and they said that several of their kids do jog. One of them is a tenth-grade girl and she jogs alone but is very careful. Some of the other ones that jog are boys. I really would

like to be able to at least bike by myself. I spent all this money on a bike and now I can't even use it. I'm going stir crazy because I can't go out!

Please! PLEASE!! At least let me do that! I'm perfectly safe on a bike.

Peep

Later that evening Kirsten joined some of the other missionaries in the library to watch a movie. Near the end, Ana burst in, hauling her large yellow backpack.

"A typhoon is headed toward the school!" she said. "It's going to hit us in twenty minutes! You have to pack up everything and move in here now!"

The SMs ran back to the apartments and grabbed their things. They moved quickly, motivated more by excitement than fear. They pushed their furniture and belongings toward the center of the rooms, then trekked with their bags back to the library.

Clouds gathered in the sky and wind beat at the windows as the group sang hymns and said prayers of safety for the school. The principal decided it was best for everyone to sleep in the administration building that night, so they divided up the rooms. Staff members with children stayed upstairs. The student missionaries lodged on the first floor.

Since there were more offices than staff, many of the rooms had fallen into disuse and hadn't been opened in quite a while. Olivia and Katherine peeked in a room. Spiders scurried across the walls. Seth looked in over their shoulders.

"There's a lot of stuff alive in there," he said. "I can kill those spiders if you want me to."

"I think we'll just go back to the library," they answered.

Meanwhile, Sterling and Alex chased a group of rats into the supply room and barricaded the crack under the door.

"Hopefully they'll stay locked up in there," Alex said.

Despite the guys' attempts, however, Kirsten heard rats chewing on the carpet throughout the night. She and Liz had ended up settling on the floor of the accounting office. The strange sounds and uncomfortable bedding made it hard to sleep, and when Kirsten awoke the next morning, she felt tired.

I need an extra boost today, Lord, she prayed. *Get me through.*

The typhoon missed the school. At the last moment, it cut around and up before resuming its original course.

* * * * *

On Tuesday afternoon Kisten got the e-mail she'd been waiting for.

Go ahead but be very alert; don't bike in lala land. You will not be perfectly safe but safer. Luv pap

I can deal with that! Kirsten journaled. She immediately e-mailed her dad back, requesting a more official-sounding letter, then sent up a quick prayer. *Praise God that I'm not confined to the campus anymore! Please just keep me safe and help me to think smart and be careful.*

* * * * *

The letter from Kirsten's dad read:

Dear Principal Fonseka,

If it meets with your approval, please allow Kirsten Wolcott to ride her bike off campus during daylight hours. She loves to do regular exercise to keep herself healthy. Thank you.

Respectfully,

Hollis Wolcott

Kirsten's dad only intended to give her permission to bike alone off campus, but Kirsten used the permission letter she gave to the principal as an excuse to jog alone too. She still started her morning jogs on campus, but once the sun came up, she spent her last fifteen minutes running on the main road. No one noticed anything amiss with the arrangement.

To further break up the monotony of their three-week break, Kirsten and the other missionaries frequently went scuba diving and snorkeling.

Hey God! Oh wow, it was so amazing yesterday getting to go snorkeling! It was just so beautiful! God, when I see all those intricate fish and my fave, the blue starfish, it just amazes me and shows me how great You are. When I can sit out in the water that is so blue it almost isn't blue, and is so beautiful it doesn't even have a color name for it, I am in total wonder of You. . . .

I'm also thankful to You that You've kept me healthy and strong. I'm a little worried about my weight, though. I'm going to start eating breakfast! Yikes, I haven't had my weight this low in awhile. I'll start working on that, but please give me the strength to do it because a lot of times I don't feel like eating or I don't want to because I'm worried about it. Help me not to obsess over it, but then also to be careful what I eat. Help me to resist eating late at night because I know that's not healthy. How about no eating after 7:00 P.M.! Help me to keep that pact with myself.

CHAPTER 08

Moon Money

In late October, school life was back in full swing.

My kids seem to be getting used to the whole "work" idea again, Kirsten wrote, *and everyone is doing pretty well! I'm really happy that Mary and the new Indian lady are doing some tutoring! It's great for my kids to get some special help!*

In addition, the student missionaries enjoyed a cultural treat: a canoe festival celebrating Yap's culture and history. School was canceled on Friday, so all the SMs drove into town. When they arrived they were greeted by a sea of colorful booths surrounding a giant platform.

For the opening session, the governor of Palau spoke about the fascinating shared history of Yap and Palau. The missionaries had heard similar versions before.

According to popular legend, long ago in the villages of Yap, people were always arguing about trade and business. They couldn't agree on a method of payment.

One night as a chief stood on the seashore looking at the full moon, an idea came to him: we should have something large, round and beautiful like the moon to use for trading—always there like the moon, something that does not break or wear out or get stolen.

The other chiefs approved, but a new problem arose: what material to use. The rocks on Yap were good for making stone paths, but lacked the durability they were looking for. The chiefs decided to send men to a new land in search of suitable material.

Up to this point, the Yapese had not sailed far from home. They didn't know whether other islands and peoples existed, though they suspected there must be life beyond their shores. Immediately men began to build outrigger canoes and weapons, while women prepared food for the voyage.

When everything was ready, the men set sail. They journeyed for over a month to the island of Palau—a distance of more than 250 miles. By the time they arrived, they'd long since run out of food. But their hardships weren't over. Startled by the arrival of explorers, the people of Palau rallied to defend their land, and the Yapese men were killed.

The Yapese chiefs grew worried when the explorers did not return home. Again, they built canoes. Again, they prepared food. Again, they set sail, hoping to find the missing warriors. Aware of the disappearance of the first explorers, the second group of Yapese explorers were prepared to fight when they landed in Palau. Sure enough, a group of warriors came out to meet them, but the Yapese won the battle and were given land as compensation. That area is now known as Angaur, Palau.

After the battle, the Yapese men traversed the island, searching for an object that was round and durable like the moon. The only thing they found was a large deposit of limestone. Satisfied, they sat down to carve. With simple tools made from wood, clamshell, and coconut rope, they perfected the shape of the moon in the stone. The carvings ranged from two to five feet in diameter. Elated at their success, the men shouted, *"Iirarai!"* which means, "This is it!" From then on, the stone money was simply called *rai*.

Rai is heavy and not easily moved. As a result, the Yapese carved a hole in the center of each stone so that they could put a tree trunk through and carry it between two men. The *rai* was then loaded onto bamboo rafts and pulled behind the canoes back to Yap.

There was great feasting and celebrating when the warriors returned home. With the *rai,* successful trading was now possible.

Ownership of *rai* is passed from one person to another, but the stone money is not necessarily moved. The value of *rai* is determined by a number of factors, including its age, size, quality, color, and shape. The most important factor, however, is the level of hardships suffered in acquisition. Consequently, the pieces of *rai* that were dropped into the ocean during transport are still in use, and are considered the most valuable.

Rai is still used to trade for land, to pay fines, and as a gift to a bride's family.

* * * * *

"Because of the use of canoes and stone money," the governor of Palau said, "the islands of Palau and Yap are forever connected."

The SMs expected a cheer from the crowd, but none came. Instead the villagers sat with patient, respectful faces turned towards the podium. The governor finished, and a group of police marched through the crowd twirling their guns.

"Oh, man, how long are these introductions going to be?" Aila asked Kirsten, but Kirsten didn't hear her. She was busy snapping pictures.

Later that afternoon the girls wandered to another area, where men, women, and children were going to perform traditional dances. Kirsten read the description of the first one in the weekend program: A Bamboo Stick Dance for Young Men and Women.

This dance is a history of the suffering endured by the
Yapese people during WWII. It tells of when the Americans

came to the island and fought against the Japanese for control. During this time, the Yapese were forced to abandon their homes and seek shelter in caves and tree trunks. The purpose of this dance is not only to tell of the past, but also to celebrate the survival of the Yapese traditions and customs in spite of such oppression.

The dancers lined up in two rows and faced each other. Each was holding a bamboo stick and wearing a multicolored grass skirt with red, green, yellow, and blue.

As the dance started, the performers twirled, tapped, and twisted. The clanking of their bamboo sticks created a steady rhythm, to which the chanter sang out the story of Yap. Kirsten didn't understand the words, but she was fascinated by the skill of the dances.

I totally want to learn how to do that, she journaled. *To see what a great workout and such amazing coordination it takes is just so awesome. One of Aila's kids danced in it, and she was the littlest one. It was amazing!*

CHAPTER 09

"Come Fill Up My Heart"

That weekend the missionaries had a potluck, but Kirsten didn't eat much.

God, I'm still struggling with the whole food thing, she journaled. *I skimp all day it seems like and then gorge myself at night. I don't understand it and don't like how I feel afterwards. I think I'm addicted to the feeling of putting food in my mouth. I don't know, though. Like I'm not sure if I'm hungry or not; I'm past the point of being able to tell. I don't listen to my body anymore, and I don't like it! Give me restraint and help me not to overeat.*

Over the next two weeks, the pace continued to pick up and Kirsten felt increasingly stressed, frazzled, and disorganized.

I felt kind of sick yesterday and I'm not sure why. But by the evening I was OK. I'm staying really busy and I get kinda frustrated because I feel like I'm doing everything. Like I shop for the food, cook it, prep it, which I love and don't mind. But sometimes peeps could offer to help prep. But then I also wash the dishes, boil the silverware, put all the dishes away, and make bread. I have other responsibilities too! Sure, I take my 40 min–1 hour "me time" to exercise, and I try to make time in the evening to get on the Internet, but come on! It's not like I have anything less to do! So I'm going on a dish strike. I'm not gonna wash or take trash out or wipe counters (except where I make a mess) or anything! I'm only gonna cook! We'll see how long it lasts. This should be interesting. Time for some other peeps to step it up!

In addition, she couldn't shake the feeling that she wasn't doing enough to get close to God.

I've been having some trouble focusing on God, she journaled. *I feel like I've been running nonstop this whole week. I feel like I don't even have time to breathe. I make time to exercise and cook and then everything pretty much is about school. I feel like sometimes my heart and mind are very far from Him. I feel like I have to do it all, fix it all, take care of it all. . . .*

For days Kirsten's mind raced continually, and she had no peace. She felt like she was failing at her attempts to do more for God. *I don't think my faith has been growing in Him. I also am not sure that I've been doing anything to help spread His gospel. I feel like I'm just kind of floating through life.*

Kirsten prayed for a solution to the chaos, and one Sabbath the answer seemed to come: perhaps she should go deeper into the Word of God. Kirsten decided that as she studied a particular passage of Scripture, she would also take time to study the cross-references and background information. That would help her know what Scripture was saying to her.

Kirsten continued to lay out her plan. Then suddenly she stopped.

Am I making this too much like an assignment, God? Are You just shaking Your head and smiling? God, I wish I could see You right now. I just want to sit on Your lap and stare at Your face and ask You myself. I just want to touch Your mighty arms holding me as I listen to Your heart beating and as my breathing slowly matches Yours. I know that I can see You in nature and in my kids, and I do! But I just want to feel Your power and Your tenderness in a different way. I want to be like a little kid in their daddy's arms. God, reach out to me today, please. And if it's Your will, help me to reach out to someone. Use me as Your hands and feet. I want to give and I want to be used, but right now I feel like I need to be filled up too. Is that selfish to think? God, please help fill me up with more so I can keep giving more. Thanks for talking with me this morning and letting me bring all my random questions, scattered thoughts, and whatever to You. I'm so glad that I can talk to You whenever and that I can be open and honest with You.

* * * * *

Over the next week and a half, Kirsten felt a greater sense of peace. *God, I'm really excited about today,* she wrote. *I feel in love with life this morning. . . Come fill up my heart with Your love and help me to be able to brighten someone's day today. Use me for Your service. God, please help me now as I read Your words. I want to be spiritually filled. Send Your Holy Spirit to come and speak to my mind as I read and study. Then please help me to have the energy and be safe when I'm on my run this morning.*

November 17 was Alex's birthday, so to celebrate the group decided to go out to Manta Ray, a boat that had been renovated into a restaurant. Eating at Manta Ray was a real treat, first because they served American food like pizza. The SMs chattered excitedly as they climbed the stairs to the top deck, overlooking the ocean.

Kirsten sat near the middle of the table, where she could hold conversations with both sides of the large group. After ordering, the talk turned to the upcoming holidays.

"What does your family usually do for Thanksgiving?" someone asked.

"In the past," Kirsten said, "we used to each take turns going around the table and saying what we're thankful for before we eat. But we haven't done that as much recently. Instead, we all draw names of our cousins and relatives and plan what we're going to get them for Christmas. Then on Christmas Eve, we gather at my grandparents' house and exchange gifts. When we were young my mom used to dress all us kids up and we'd act out the Christmas story, but we haven't done that as much recently either."

"That sounds cool," someone said.

"Yeah. My parents are actually coming to Yap this year for Christmas," Kirsten said. "They're going to spend two weeks visiting me, and my dad's going to do some missionary dental work."

Just a few more weeks until she could embrace them.

CHAPTER 10

November 19

Kirsten woke up to a rainy darkness, so she decided to have devotions before running. She opened her computer and journaled.

Hey God. Again, before I start I'd like to praise You for a new day of life. I'm thankful for the rain because it makes things cooler, but it's really hard for things to dry, and it's hard for my kids to be able to play outside when it's so wet.

I'm so thankful that it's Thursday! This week has been kind of rough. God, I love my kids and I don't want to see any of them go, but Tanya has really been testing me. God, I don't know how I can show love to her! I need Your help knowing what to do. Impress me as to how I can get closer to her.

Thanks so much that I'm not feeling as sleepy this morning as I have been some other mornings. I've been really blessed by all of Aila's worships and I'm very thankful for them. Please help me as I prepare to do worships. I feel very out of control right now. I need Your help, Your organization, and most of all, Your peace. Help keep me safe today as I jog and please help the rain to stop.

Thanks so much for little Yap and for the chance to teach. I'm so happy it's town day, even though I have a lot to do. Come and fill my heart today. I need Your help to be a good teacher.

Kirsten flipped open her Bible and read from Matthew 26. Jesus and the disciples have just eaten the Passover dinner together and walked across the Kidron Valley to the Garden of Gethsemane. When they arrive, Jesus takes His three closest disciples away and asks them to pray. Drops of blood streak His face like sweat. He knows what's coming; He's dreading the pain and separation from His Father. Every sin that was, is, and ever will be is being placed upon Him. Walking farther away from the three, He falls on His face and pleads, "My Father, if it is possible, let this cup pass from me; nevertheless, not as I will, but as you will" (verse 39).

Kirsten stopped. *I can't even imagine it,* she wrote. *And yet He was willing. I just think that's so amazing. It's really easy to pray that God's will be done, but it's so much harder to actually do it. God, Jesus had such a strong relationship with You that He was truly able to pray that and really mean it.*

She finished reading the section, paying special attention to Jesus' warning to keep watch and pray. *My goal for today is to stay extra vigilant,* she told God. *I want to focus on You more. Today I want to be positive and pray before I lose my self-control. I want to show my kids Your love today. God, I don't want to sleep and let the devil slip in. Please guard my heart. Thanks, God. Amen.*

By this time the rain had let up, so Kirsten fastened on her headlight and went out alone for her morning jog.

* * * * *

Principal Fonseka had noticed Kirsten was absent from morning worship, but he—and everyone else—assumed she was on supervision duty. Each week the teachers took turns standing outside to watch the children who arrived early. After worship, everyone went to their classes. The principal headed to his office. What he saw made him stop: Liz was watching the children.

"Where's Kirsten?" he asked.

"I don't know. Wasn't she in worship with you?"

"No."

"Let's go check the apartment."

As she walked, Liz wondered why she hadn't seen Kirsten all morning. Normally, Kirsten would have come back and gotten ready for school after running.

They climbed the steps and opened the door.

"Kirsten?" Liz called as they went in. No answer. She looked in the rooms and checked the bathroom.

"She's not here."

* * * * *

Principal Fonseka returned to the administration building and immediately called the police, the Guam-Micronesia Mission (GMM), and Kirsten's parents.

The Wolcott family had just finished a late dinner in their Virginia home when the phone rang. It was 8:00 P.M. in Virginia, 9:00 A.M. in Yap.

"Kirsten didn't show up for class this morning," the voice on the line said. "But you're the one who gave her permission to exercise alone off campus."

"No, we didn't," Karen said, as she frantically motioned for Hollis to pick up. He got on the line, and the principal repeated the news.

"What can we do?" Hollis asked.

"At this point, nothing," the principal said. "I've notified the GMM, and we're going to look around the school. They will let you know if there is any other news."

"What should we do?" Karen asked Hollis when they got off the phone.

"Pray," he said.

3—L. K.

* * * * *

While the principal made phone calls in his office, Liz waited outside with Katherine and Miss Mary, filling them in on the few details she knew. When the principal returned, the four said a prayer. Then, through heavy rain, the principal and registrar left campus. They drove up and down the road in both directions, as far as Tom's Store on one side and the stone money on the other, but found nothing.

* * * * *

The 9:10 period was just beginning.

"It's time to get started," Lorraine said. The chattering gradually died off as groups of students gravitated toward their desks.

"Let's have a word of prayer," Lorraine said. Suddenly, a boy raised his hand.

"Yes?" Lorraine asked.

"Miss, are we still having class despite what's happened? Aren't we going to look for the missing teacher?"

"What are you talking about?" Lorraine asked.

Just then she saw a police car pull in front of the administration building. Three officers stepped out. The students rushed to the windows.

"OK, everyone, back to your seats," Lorraine said. "Come on, back to your seats. It's time for us to start." The administration hadn't said anything to her about a missing teacher.

The students dragged themselves back to their desks, but their eyes remained riveted on the windows. "Miss," they kept saying, "what about the missing teacher?"

Finally, Lorraine stopped writing on the chalkboard and set her book on the desk. "All right, what's this news you've heard?"

The students leaned forward. "Haven't you heard? A teacher is missing! She went out running and didn't come back."

Immediately Lorraine thought of Kirsten and Ana. But she'd seen both of them the previous evening. *It must just be a rumor.*

The students kept talking.

"It was the second-grade teacher," they said. "She went jogging off campus this morning and never came back."

Lorraine's heartbeat quickened, and she felt cold all over. *Kirsten.*

"Well," she said, trying to remain calm, "let's offer up a word of prayer, and I'm sure everything will be fine."

She led the class in prayer and resumed the lesson. All along, she prayed frantically inside. *Please let her just be injured somewhere. Let her just be hurt, or delayed, or let it just be that she took shelter under cover somewhere until it stopped raining.*

But Lorraine knew Kirsten wasn't that kind of person. She was never late. She was never missing.

A few minutes later, the registrar came in. "One of the teachers is missing," he said. "The police received a call that a man from jail was spotted drunk and riding a bicycle in the direction of the school early this morning."

Goosebumps spread across Lorraine's flesh.

"Keep everyone inside," the registrar told her. "But be prepared, because we might form search parties later."

The students erupted. "Let us help you look!" they pleaded. "Nothing will happen if you wait for the police to form a search team!"

"Besides, we know this area better! We'll have a better chance of finding her."

"No," the registrar said. "It could be dangerous, and we don't want to lose anyone. Stay here and I'll be back later."

At 10:00 A.M., the registrar returned. "Boys, follow me," he said. "We're forming search parties."

The girls begged to go along.

"Only the boys," he said.

* * * * *

Seth tried to keep his students together, but their eagerness pulled them in all directions. After searching the campus and finding no trace of Kirsten, several groups of high schoolers were authorized to look off campus. His was one of them. It was still raining on and off, coming down in sudden, violent torrents—then vanishing. The sky remained strangely bright and sunny.

"Don't go far," the principal had instructed, but Seth's students rushed ahead of him. They walked, ran, and scurried chaotically from tree to tree, bush to bush, calling, "Kirsten! Kiiiiiirrrrsten!"

Soon they were far ahead of Seth, past the approved searching bounds. They went all the way to Tom's Store. Still, they found nothing. On the way back one of the boys saw something in the tall grass. He walked closer to take a look. There, between two coconut trees, was Kirsten's naked body.

* * * * *

Liz was lingering near the administration building when a swarm of cars pulled up. The people that exited spoke animatedly in Yapese. Suddenly, a woman turned to Liz and said, "Do you want to go? Get in the car with me."

They must have found her, Liz thought. *I better go in case Kirsten's hurt and needs to go to the hospital. She'll want someone with her.*

She jumped in and they tore out of the dirt driveway, up the road toward Tom's Store. On the way, Liz saw a group of students walking back to the school. Their blank stares and ashen faces deepened her concern.

When they got to the scene, the woman parked on the opposite side of the road. Liz sprang out and rushed toward the people clustered near the trees. Suddenly, a man stepped in front of her and thrust out his arm to hold her back. His eyes held a look of warning.

"Don't go over there," he said.

She looked at him wide-eyed, then burst into tears.

* * * * *

Back at the school, the registrar had told all the teachers to come to the office for an emergency meeting. Lorraine put a student in charge of her class and left. When she got to the office, she saw the principal, the pastor, and Miss Mary talking intently. *What's going on?* Lorraine asked with her eyes, but no one seemed to want to answer. She moved across the lobby, where she saw other teachers.

"What happened?" they asked each other, but no one knew.

A phone rang. A woman answered. Suddenly, she put her hand over her mouth. "They found her . . . they found her body—" She shook her head and broke into tears.

At that moment, Liz arrived and ran toward Katherine. The two embraced and sank to the ground in tears. Aila stood expressionless. Olivia sat down and pulled her knees up to her chest and rocked back and forth. The loudest wails came from the principal's office, where Miss Mary clung to the desk. It was noon.

* * * * *

"Should we continue with classes?" Principal Fonseka asked the pastor.

"No," he said. "Gather everyone and tell them to go to the chapel."

By the time the second-graders walked in, the rest of the school had already assembled. Makea seemed confused, so Lorraine took her by the hand to lead her to the front. Makea looked up.

"Am I going to see my teacher again?" she asked.

Lorraine gulped. She couldn't bring herself to answer.

"Am I going to see my teacher again?"

"The pastor has some very important news to tell us."

"But am I going to see my teacher again? Am I going to see her tomorrow in class?"

By this time they were near the front, so Lorraine ignored the question and helped Makea get seated. The pastor started to speak.

"This morning," he said, and went on to explain the events, but used Ana's name instead of Kirsten's.

Startled, the principal rushed to the front to make the correction. The pastor started his message again.

"This morning the second grade teacher, Kirsten, went missing and was found dead. You should understand, though, that there's a reason for this."

"Stop!" Makea shrieked. "Stop! Stop! I don't want to hear this about my teacher!"

The pastor turned and looked down at Makea.

"Well, you have to hear this," he said.

"No! I don't want to hear this about my teacher!" she yelled back at him.

Someone moved in to calm Makea.

The pastor continued.

"Everything happens for a reason," he said. "We may not understand it, but it's God's will. We must just keep praying and remember that God loves us and will protect us. We must put our trust in Him."

An eighth-grader burst from her seat in the back.

"If God will protect us, then why didn't He protect Kirsten?"

The room fell silent. Everyone wondered the same question.

* * * * *

After they'd received the initial call from the principal, Hollis and Karen Wolcott hadn't said much. They were both thinking the same thing: *Kirsten is never late for class.*

That evening Hollis dialed a few numbers to ask others to pray. Karen called her relatives and tearfully told them what was happening.

She tried to convince herself that everything would be OK, but one word kept repeating itself in her head. *Rape.*

Several hours later, the Wolcotts still hadn't heard anything, so Hollis called the school. Miss Mary answered.

"This is Hollis Wolcott calling," he said. "Any news about Kirsten?"

Missy Mary burst into tears. Hollis's heart froze.

"Kirsten's body was just found," sobbed the woman. "We can't tell you anything because we don't know. There was no blood on the scene. It's possible she died from natural causes."

Karen stared at Hollis. She knew Kirsten hadn't died of natural causes.

PART 02

CHAPTER 11

Family

"Are we still headed in the right direction?" I ask my friend, who has agreed to accompany me on this trip to Virginia. She consults the GPS. According to Google Maps, the gravel road should curve left and lead us to the edge of the Rappahannock River where Kirsten's grandparents live. Instead it ends abruptly between two houses and a ditch. We stare at the screen, stumped. The pulsating blue dot is at rest.

"I guess I'll call," I say and dial the number.

"Hello?" a voice answers on the other end. It's Tove Oster, Kirsten's mormor.

"Hi, it's Rainey Park," I say. I explain that we're close by, but lost.

"Vell, tell me vhere you are," she says in her thick Danish accent.

I name a couple of roads, but she says she's never heard of them before. She passes off the phone to her husband.

"Hello," says a deeper voice. I rename the roads, but with no luck. Now I'm starting to feel nervous. Are we far off?

"Just go back to the 606 and I'll meet you there," he says, "You can look for my car."

In muffled tones I hear him turn to his wife and ask, "What does my car look like?"

"It's red," she says.

"I know it's red, but what kind of model and year is it?"

More muffled sounds as they try to remember.

"It's OK," I interrupt. "I'm sure I'll see you." Just in case, I tell him I'm driving a white Chrysler Pacifica.

There's hesitation on his end.

To clarify, I add, "It looks like a white minivan." As I say it, I grimace. I hate when people refer to my vehicle as a minivan. But it works.

"OK," he replies in more confident tones. "A white minivan."

"Yes," I grimace again.

I hang up and drive back to the 606. A few minutes later, a red Saturn pulls up; a small man grins and waves at us. His eyes are all at once deeply sad and twinkling with mischievousness. Something about his newsboy hat and mannerisms make him look as if he's just stepped out of a sidewalk café in Europe. All he needs is the newspaper and a coffee cup. He motions for us to follow him.

A few minutes down the road, we make a left turn, and his car suddenly stops.

"What's he doing?" I ask Vanessa. Niels gets out of the car and walks toward us.

"You see that sign over there?" he asks, pointing to a green aluminum strip nailed to a tree.

DR. N. OSTER.

"That's me!" he says, grinning mischievously. Then he turns and drives off.

* * * * *

Kirsten's family has a long history in Virginia. Her grandparents—Niels and Tove Oster moved to the area in 1966, shortly after the Tappahannock Seventh-day Adventist hospital first opened. For more than thirty-five years, Niels worked there as a surgeon.

Then, at the age of sixty-six, he moved to Africa to be a medical missionary. During the twelve years he was away, Tove stayed planted in Tappahannock, close to her grandchildren, including Kirsten.

As I sit in the Osters' cozy yellow sunroom, buried under handmade quilts and gazing out the windows at the Rappahannock River, Tove shares memories of Kirsten.

"Kirsten and I had a special relationship," she says. "Of course, I love all my grandchildren, but I always felt that Kirsten and I were most alike. We thought similarly, you know?

"She came over here a lot and we'd garden together or cook. Sometimes she'd come in the door and say, 'Let's have fun, Grandma!' In the summer she painted our deck, cared for our garden, taught Vacation Bible School at the church and painted the walls at her aunt's daycare center in the evenings. Sometimes I'd say to her, 'Kirsten, slow down.' But she said, 'It's all right, Grandma. I like doing these things. I'm OK. I can do it.' And she always did. She was so helpful."

While she talks I glance at Niels, who's sitting in an armchair in the corner. His legs are crossed, and his elbow is resting on one knee while simultaneously propping up his head. I can tell he's listening, but his eyes are far away. His forehead crinkles and his face puckers, as if he's about to weep. All at once, he looks both age two and age ninety.

"My dad had such a hard time when he found out," Karen had told me earlier over the phone. "I think it's because he served for twelve years in the most remote areas of Africa and was never hurt. Kirsten was gone for less than four months and was killed. That's so hard for him to understand. The evening he heard the news he kept saying, 'It should have been me. It should have been me.' "

My attention quickly returns to Tove, who's pulled out family albums and programs from Kirsten's funeral.

"I often wonder about this picture," Tove says, holding a photo of Kirsten standing in an open Tennessee field. Her face is tilted toward the sky, and her arms are stretched wide, as if embracing the whole world.

"It's such an interesting position, you know?" she says, mimicking Kirsten's open arms. "I've never seen her do that before, and I often wonder what is meant by it. It's like she wanted to do everything, like she wanted to take in the whole world."

Tove stares at the picture a little longer.

"Sometimes I wonder if she knew she wasn't going to live long." Her voice trails off. "But of course, she couldn't have known that . . ."

* * * * *

That afternoon I drive to the Tappahannock Seventh-day Adventist school, where Karen Wolcott teaches. I find her in her kindergarten classroom cleaning up after a day of school. When Karen sees me, she smiles, a Kirsten kind of smile.

"You must be Rainey," she says, extending her hand.

"It's nice to meet you," I say, noticing how her wavy black hair is so similar to Kirsten's.

"Should we go for a drive?" she asks.

Karen takes me on a tour of the town, pointing out meaningful places: the hospital that first brought their family to Tappahannock, the church where Kirsten sang with the choir, their first home, the daycare center where Kirsten worked.

"Kirsten loved Tappahannock. This is where she wanted to live when she finished college. She always asked me, 'Mom, what if the person I marry doesn't want to live here?' And I'd tell her, 'Well, Kirsten, you don't have to worry about that right now.' But she wanted her dad to build her a house here like he built ours."

I'm surprised at how easily Karen talks about Kirsten, but the tone of conversation changes as we near Hollis's office.

"Kirsten's body came home on Thanksgiving Day. All the family was gathered at my parents' house, and after we ate our meal we just sat around, waiting for the phone call that said she arrived. In the morning, we got the message that her plane had made it to Houston, but they were refusing to let her through customs since they didn't have the proper staff that day. We immediately called Louis Torres [president of the Guam-Micronesia Mission of Seventh-day Adventists], who was accompanying her body home, and told him what we had learned. He was sitting on the plane waiting for it to take off and no one had told him.

"As soon as we called he got off that plane and went to talk to the airport staff. He said, 'There's a family waiting for their daughter to come home, and you have to let her through.' So they did.

"A few hours later we got another call saying Kirsten had arrived. Hollis went with the hearse driver to pick up the body from the airport. I think that was hard, but at the same time, important for him. The last time he saw her he was dropping her off at an airport; he didn't expect to pick her up this way.

"I was a little worried about what Kirsten would look like. Many people forewarned me that they may not have been able to care for her body properly on Yap and that I might not want to see her, but before Kirsten got home, a woman from Guam e-mailed me and told me she saw Kirsten. 'She looks like an angel,' the woman wrote. She said it looked like someone took time to wash and comb her hair, and that she was wearing a pretty purple skirt. I was so relieved.

"Hollis didn't want to see the body, because he wants to remember Kirsten the way she was, but I wanted to see. I wasn't sure if I could handle it; I wasn't even sure if I was going to do it, right up to the moment that I was standing outside the door, but then I did. And then, once I was there . . ."

Tears roll down Karen's face.

"I had the hardest time leaving, because I knew it was the last time I'd ever see her. I must have sat in that room for at least half an hour."

Karen pauses to catch her breath, then tentatively resumes.

"Kirsten did look nice. You couldn't tell there were wounds on her, except for a small bruise on her cheek. There was a scarf tied around her neck, which covered the wounds there. Later I asked for the scarf, and they let me keep it.

"We had the funeral service that Sunday, which was really important to me, because I didn't want it happening the following weekend, on her birthday.

"I know this sounds irrational, but as I was sitting there in the front row at the funeral, I kept having all of these thoughts like, *What if Kirsten's not really dead? What if she's alive and she starts banging on the lid of the coffin, or it opens up and she comes out? After all, Jesus has the power to raise her again.*

"Anyways, many people don't know this, but we had Kirsten cremated."

"What did you do with her ashes?" I ask.

"Nothing yet. They're just sitting on a shelf in her bedroom. Hollis wants to scatter some on the river, but I just don't know how I feel about that.

"Anyways," she says, "why don't we go inside and see if Hollis is ready?"

* * * * *

We walk inside the dental office where Hollis works.

Hollis bounds from the back wearing scrubs and a headlight. "Open up!" he says cheerfully, flashing the light in the direction of my mouth. I obey and say, "Ahhh."

"Looks good in there!" he says. We have a more formal introduction and discuss dinner options.

"Just give me a few minutes to finish up with this patient, and then I'll be ready," he says.

Half an hour later, we arrive at one of Kirsten's favorite restaurants— a Chinese place across town.

"How'd the visit with my parents go?" Karen asks.

"It was wonderful," I answer. "They were so warm and kind."

"I'm glad. I think your visit probably did my mom a lot of good. She was having such a hard time after Kirsten's death that I was really worried about her. We're on a potluck rotation together, and one day she said to me, 'You know, I'm getting too old for this. I can't do as much anymore and it's a lot of work to cook on Sabbath. I think I'd like to be taken off the potluck rotation.'

"I didn't tell her this, but in my head I thought, *Well, you have to cook on Sabbath anyways, Mom. What's the big deal?*

"But instead I just said, 'Well, how about you stay on, but I'll just give you the light stuff, like bread and salad?'

"A few weeks later my mom called again, sounding completely different. She said, 'You'll never believe what happened.' She told me that one of the chaplains from Southern printed off all the messages that people had written on their Web site about Kirsten— all thirty-eight pages of them—and mailed them to her. She and my dad started reading a few every day, and she said it made such a difference in their spirits.

" 'I'm starting to see Kirsten's death in a different light,' she said. 'Did you ever know you had such a wonderful daughter?'

"I said, 'Well, Mom, I've always thought she was pretty special, but until I started reading these messages, no, I didn't.'

"Later that week she called me again and said, 'How about for potluck this week I make a roast?' And I said, 'Mom, I thought you said you were getting tired. That's a lot of work, and I don't want you to have to do all that.' "

Tove replied with a laugh, "Oh, don't you know, Karen? I'm getting younger every day!"

* * * * *

That evening the Wolcotts insist we spend the next few nights with them rather than pay for a hotel.

"Just come pick up the key while I'm at school tomorrow, and you can go over and get your stuff settled," Karen says.

"Are you sure?" I ask. They insist.

The first thing I see upon entering the Wolcott house are blue Danish dishes hanging above the kitchen, just like at the Osters'. The living room is narrow but cozy, with a wooden staircase nestled in the corner. Beneath it are a grand piano and Kirsten's harp, which she named Isabella. I walk over and stroke the red velvet cover. I consider taking it off but don't feel ready.

Instead I ascend the staircase, stopping to look at each picture along the way: Kirsten as a little girl with chubby cheeks and dark bangs; Kirsten posing with her brothers at each Christmas throughout the years; Kirsten at the beach with a group of friends. And then there's Kirsten on the deck of a boat, smiling in one of the last pictures ever taken of her. It's framed with an Adventist mission flag.

Kirsten's room is painted red, her favorite color. Light streams in from high windows and illuminates a row of porcelain dolls atop her bookcase, along with fossils and shells she's collected from the river. The bunk bed is covered with pictures, newspaper clippings, and boxes of mail the Wolcotts have received since Kirsten's death. I pick one up and read.

> Dear Wolcott family,
> I have never met Kirsten, but today I ran a 5K for her. Every time I felt like giving up, I thought of how if she were still here, she would give anything to have one more jog, and it kept me going strong. She will be missed. I hope to see her again one day.

I pick up another.

> Kirsten has inspired me to do my best in all things, to

live my life in full dedication and service to God and His children. Not only has my life been changed by Kirsten's, but many other people's lives have been and will be changed. Though she is asleep for now, she continues to do the work of God, and the devil cannot stop that. Take hope in knowing a time will come when she will live forever. I pray for you daily. My heart breaks for you.

There are hundreds more letters, but for now I leave the box and look for Kirsten's journal from Yap. Karen has already told me where it is and given me permission to read it. I find it on a small shelf under Kirsten's desk. I pick it up and smell it—my instinct with all books—then brush my hand across the soft suede cover.

This was Kirsten's journal in Yap, I think. *It's the last record of her thoughts and experiences.*

With anticipation I take the book down to the living room and settle into a chair. I open it and read the first entry.

May 27, 2009

Dear God, Why haven't I heard back yet? I don't understand! What is taking so long? I already went through the whole ordeal of having to get a doctor's note about my anorexia and stuff. I finally got Dr. Kahler to send it if I promised to cut back on exercise. I've done that, but nothing's happened yet. God, I need to know! Do they want me? Isn't this Your will? OK, well, I'm giving it to You. I can't stress out about this. Give me Your peace—fill me with it! I'm still getting stuff ready, so I'll keep going forward until I hear something else. I'll keep You posted! Love Ya, Kirsten.

By the time the Wolcotts get home, I'm halfway through the journal. I set it aside and help them get ready for dinner. Hollis is making a navy bean soup.

"Have you read Kirsten's journal?" I ask as I place glasses on the table. I already know Karen has.

"Naw, I suppose I will someday, but I haven't yet."

While the beans simmer, Hollis pulls out pictures from their last family vacation.

"This is our house down in Hatteras," he tells me. "We've had it for years—ever since Kirsten was about two, I think—and whenever we go there we do a little work on it."

In the pictures, Kirsten is helping her dad install new doors.

"They worked on a lot of projects together," Karen says. "Kirsten's always been a Daddy's girl."

"Yep, she's my little Peeper," Hollis says. "That's my nickname for her."

"Where'd it come from?" I ask.

"Where *did* it come from?" Hollis repeats the question, straining to remember.

"Oh, I know," he says suddenly. "Wasn't it that old commercial? Yeah, that's right."

Hollis tells me about a telephone service commercial where a little boy is sitting on the steps of his home, sad that his brother has gone off to college.

"Just think," his friend tries to comfort him. "Nobody will call you Peeper anymore."

"Yeah," the boy says sullenly. Just then his mom comes out on the porch and says, "David, your brother's on the phone. He wants to talk to you."

David's face lights up. He races inside and picks up the telephone.

"Hi, Brian!" he says.

"Hey, Peeper! How you doin', kid?"

They both smile as the Bell System logo flashes across the screen and gentle voices sing, "Reach out and touch someone."

"Yeah," Hollis says, eyes lingering on Kirsten's picture. "She's my little Peeper."

* * * * *

Later Karen and I go up to Kirsten's room to search for more journals.

"Wow, I've never seen this before," Karen says. I look over to where she's sitting, holding a scrapbook in her lap.

"This is a wedding portfolio Kirsten had to make for Bible class her senior year of high school."

The pages are filled with pasted pictures of wedding dresses, party favors, and tuxedos. Light blue paper matches the seashell theme that Kirsten chose.

Karen flips another page and comes to a list. "How ironic," she says, after reading to the bottom. "Everyone Kirsten wanted to play a special part in her wedding did exactly the part she chose, except it was at her funeral."

When we finish looking at the scrapbook, Karen slips it back into the shelf and picks up an old shoebox.

Inside is a thin green journal with a picture of a wheelbarrow and flowers on the front. It's dated May 31 to June 30, 1999—Kirsten's earliest journal. When she wrote in this, Kirsten was eleven years old, on a trip with her mormor and cousin to visit relatives in Norway, Denmark, and Iceland. We read the first entry.

Today I was so excited when we borded the plane. I was nerves, too. Once we got in the air I was fine but hungry. We got food at 10:30 but it was not vegitarin. At 11:00 mormor got her supper it was vegitarian. It was lazanya and brochaly. Mormor let us have some. It was delishis! . . . This is the longest trip I've ever been on. At night I saw a lighting storm it was asome. Well my eyes hert so I'm going to stop good night! I love you!

A few pages later is a little note Karen wrote in the top of the journal for Kirsten to discover on her trip.

Kirsten, I love you + miss you. Have a great time. Be kind + helpful + you'll have fun! Love, Mommy

Karen sighs.

* * * * *

After finding five more journals, Karen and I take a break. She sits at Kirsten's desk. I remain on the floor, studying the trinkets on Kirsten's bookshelves. Near the bottom I notice a white figurine of Jesus. He's smiling with arms outstretched, palms turned upward toward heaven. It reminds me of the picture of Kirsten standing in the open field.

"Behind that is the box with Kirsten's ashes," Karen says. I look, expecting an ornately carved box or delicate urn; instead I see a deep red velvet bag, like the cover on Kirsten's harp.

"You can open it and look, if you'd like."

"Have you?" I ask.

"No, I haven't yet."

I feel strange being the first one to open the bag. "Are you sure?" I ask.

"Yes, go ahead."

I move the figurine and lift the bag off the shelf.

"Wow, this is surprisingly heavy," I say.

"How much do you think it weighs?" Karen asks.

"Not sure," I answer, moving it up and down. I hand it to her and she does the same.

"At least ten pounds." She hands it back to me. I set it on the floor and loosen the drawstrings, then pull out a black plastic box. Karen and I both stare at it for a minute. I don't think it's what either one of us expected.

"Wow," she says. "That's pretty plain."

She picks it up and looks for markings, but the only thing we see is a string of numbers lightly etched into one of the edges.

"I wonder how you open it," Karen says. She turns it over and begins prying on the top. The lid holds fast.

* * * * *

"Do you ever feel guilty," I ask the Wolcotts later. "For writing the permission letter saying Kirsten could exercise off campus?"

"No," Karen answers immediately. "For one thing, we didn't give her permission to run off campus. We gave her permission to bike. The day she was murdered she was running, so it wouldn't have made a difference."

"Besides," Hollis adds. "I think there's a pretty good chance he was stalking her. He would've gotten her some time or other. It wouldn't have made a difference."

Karen speaks up. "Sometimes I do ask, 'Kirsten, why'd you have to break a rule? Why did you do that?' She was such an obedient girl that when we first told people what happened, no one believed Kirsten broke a rule. They all said she must have been dragged off campus. But it's like my sister told me. She said, 'You know, Karen, in the end it doesn't matter if she broke the rule or not. Everyone has a right to exercise; no one has a right to murder.' "

* * * * *

My last evening in Virginia, many family members gather at Kirsten's aunt's house to watch home videos. We start with one of Kirsten at the age of two, playing in the front yard with her two older brothers on a hot summer day. She swings contentedly while they run around as boys do, throwing sticks and climbing the edges of the play set. The family laughs delightedly at how cute Kirsten looks and how funny her brothers are.

"Her brothers took it so hard," Karen says. Scott is at Walla Walla University in Washington, where he's attending college and Nathan is working in a different part of Virginia, so neither are here to watch the videos with us. "I think they feel a sense of responsibility, like somehow as her brothers they should have been able to protect her."

In another video, Kirsten is now three or four—sitting in Sabbath School with her dad and a circle of children.

"Oh, that's Chris Brown!" her aunt says.

"You don't mean Chris Brown the singer, do you?" I ask.

"Yeah—that's him! His family lives around here and he used to come to Sabbath School at our church."

Later we see him again at a birthday party at Kirsten's house.

We put in the next video and watch eight-year-old Kirsten plunk piano keys with determination at a recital.

"That isn't Kirsten, is it?" someone asks. "Wow! She looks so different."

We watch more videos—Christmases, birthday parties, family get-togethers. Each scene evokes a series of comments from the family members.

"Oh, is that . . . ?"

"Oh, remember when . . . ?"

"Oh, listen to her talk . . ."

Afterward we linger in the living room as the family continues to smile and reminisce. When the conversation finally slows, I say my goodbyes and walk out into the crisp night air. The stars shine brightly above and I shiver a little, even as warmth and light still emanate behind me. It's been a special trip to Kirsten's home.

Next, I'm on my way to Yap.

CHAPTER 12

Return to Yap

Jet-lagged, I wake up early. Muggy air clings to me. I kick off the sheet and turn over in what used to be Kirsten's bed. Her journal is in my suitcase across the room.

As soon as I see the sun rising, I decide to go for a walk on campus. The dogs that often followed Kirsten greet me as I descend the rickety wooden stairs from her apartment.

"Good morning, Polgus," I say. Red dirt clings to his shaggy white fur. Trailing Polgus are Frankie and a black puppy born shortly after Kirsten's death. The dogs patter behind as I walk along the narrow sidewalk.

"Ow!" I cry suddenly. My foot is caught in a section of broken cement. Pulling it free, I tread more cautiously.

After crossing the basketball court and a small field, I reach a wooden deck overlooking an ocean inlet. A large tree hangs over it, offering shade from the hot morning. I sit on the bench and take in the scenery.

A hundred yards of low-growing plants and mangrove trees separate me from the water. All is still and quiet, except for a breeze rustling its way towards the ocean and a few roosters crowing in the distance. I understand why Kirsten felt so safe here. I consider walking on the road for a bit and exploring off campus, but another thought objects.

Don't be foolish. Wait for the others.

* * * * *

The mix of missionaries on the island now is different from when Kirsten served. While most of the original group remained in Yap, three left after Kirsten's death—and three others have since filled their spots.

"I don't think I can do this anymore," Liz told the Fonsekas on the day of Kirsten's murder.

Miss Mary gave her a concerned look. "Come inside so we can talk about this." She and her husband led Liz into the principal's office.

The Fonsekas listened as Liz explained her reasons. "It's not that I'm fearful," she said. "I just don't feel like I can go on teaching. Normal life is already exhausting here, and I've been giving it all I have. I don't think I can do that anymore. I want to go home."

The Fonsekas drew in a sharp breath. It had been a hard day for everyone; they didn't want Liz to make her decision in a rush.

"Please don't decide yet," Principal Fonseka said. "Think about it, and pray. At least wait until the people come from the Guam-Micronesia Mission. Then give us your final decision." Liz agreed.

That Sabbath was hard for all the SMs, but especially for Liz. Every song at church made her think of Kirsten, who always hummed when she worked and cooked. Liz looked around for comfort, and a woman from the church approached.

"You need to be strong," she said. "Everyone can tell you are being really weak." It took everything Liz had not to burst into tears. *I can't do this anymore,* she thought. *I can't.*

* * * * *

When school resumed on Monday, everyone struggled to make it through the regular routine. The missionaries, drained from a weekend of memorial services, tears, and interviews with the FBI, had no motivation to teach. The students, filled with confusion, anxiety, doubt, and fear, had no motivation to learn.

In some ways, the presence of the Guam-Micronesian Mission officials helped, but in other ways it made things worse.

"Come on girls—no smiles? Why the sad faces?" a conference official teased. Katherine realized his intentions were probably innocent, but his mannerisms frustrated her and the others.

Everything is so fresh, Katherine thought. *And yet here you are flying in from Guam where everything is OK and trying to push your optimism on us.*

One of the conference officials listened intently as the two girls shared their feelings. "I feel like no one is allowing us just to be sad," Olivia told him. She and Katherine wanted to go home, but they weren't sure it was the right thing to do. They knew Liz had already decided to leave. If they left, what would happen to the school? Who would teach fifth grade? Who would teach science? Who would be vice principal for the high school? They felt a burden to stick it out for the kids, but at the same time, they were struggling with their own grief.

"On one hand, I'm thinking this is what being a missionary is about," Katherine said, "trusting in God, that He will get us through. It's not like I want to abandon being a missionary. But at the same time, another opportunity for mission service has opened up closer to home, and I feel like that's where I need to be right now."

When Japhet De Oliveira, the girls' chaplain from Andrews University called, Katherine and Olivia shared their feelings with him.

"Yes, you could stay," he said. "But when you leave you might be drained to a point that it would be much harder to recover from. I will support whatever decision you make, but I strongly encourage you to come home."

The following Wednesday the three girls packed their belongings, and the principal and his wife drove them to the airport. Miss Mary hugged them goodbye, while Principal Fonseka stood silently. The girls boarded the plane and left. They felt simultaneously relieved to be going home and sad that they were leaving on such bad terms.

What will happen to the school now? Katherine wondered.

* * * * *

To the Fonsekas' relief, three new missionaries arrived in January. Gus and Andrea were recent graduates from Southern. Scott was a sophomore at Pacific Union College in California.

"What made you decide to come to Yap?" I ask each of them.

Gus answers first. "I was sitting in Southern's vespers service the Friday after Kirsten's death, and when President Bietz started talking about it, I heard this voice that said, 'Go.'" He punches a fist into a flattened palm for emphasis.

"I knew it was the Holy Spirit. I thought, this is like a battle, but it's spiritual warfare. You need to send reinforcements in immediately, or the area is permanently weakened. The next Monday I went into the missions office and filled out my paperwork. Then after graduating in December, I flew straight out here."

It's Andrea's turn. "Part of the reason I came is because of Gus," she says, quietly and composed. "I was working in the missions office when Gus came in, and I helped him fill out his paperwork. For the next several nights, I had trouble sleeping because I kept thinking about Kirsten and what happened to her. Even though I didn't know her, it mattered to me. I have a mind that tends to want to process things.

"Whenever tragedy happens, everyone wants to *do* something.

They want to fix something that's broken, but oftentimes, there's nothing you can do. I knew I couldn't fix it, but I could do something good. This was a rare opportunity.

"That evening my dad called me and asked what my plans were for the following semester. At first I hesitated to answer, because I didn't want to ruin my parents' Thanksgiving by telling them I was thinking of going to Yap, but then he said, 'Are you going to travel? Maybe go to Yap?' "

"Why did he ask that?" I ask.

"Oh, my dad knows me.

"Still, I didn't want to make up my mind fully, so I decided to wait until after the funeral. I was asked to drive one of the vans up from Southern to Virginia. I didn't know what it would be like to see her parents and see them missing their daughter, but many things gave me courage."

"Like what?" I ask.

"Mostly her parents. How they believed in what she was doing. How they believed it needed to continue. Over the next month, everything fell into place, and by January I was in Yap, teaching Kirsten's class."

"How did you feel about taking over Kirsten's class?"

"At first I felt intimidated when I looked at Kirsten's lesson plans. It seemed like she was always doing new things with the kids. She worked hard to engage them, and I think that really helped set up the momentum so they were ready to learn when I got here.

"It sounds weird to say I feel like God wanted me here, because I wouldn't be here if it weren't for what happened to Kirsten. And yet, I feel like He did."

Scott wasn't a student at Southern and he didn't know Kirsten, but he is a long-time friend of Sterling and Alex. In fact, the two had originally invited him to go with them when they first signed up to be missionaries in Yap. But Scott said No. He had too many nursing classes to finish, and he wanted to stay on track. Everything changed in November when he got an e-mail from Sterling and Alex sharing the news about Kirsten and asking him again to join them.

"Within, like, ten days of making my decision," Scott says, "I was on a plane to Yap."

* * * * *

By 9:30 A.M., the guys are up and ready to go to jail ministry. My traveling partner, Tyler, and I accompany them. The school used to send missionaries every other Sunday, but in more recent years they haven't. Since Kirsten's death, the missionaries have started the ministry back up. The van swerves left and right around potholes, and I cling to my seat.

"Last week Scott got a ticket for driving without his license," one of the guys tells me. "But what's really funny is that on the ticket there were a whole list of possible offenses, and it doesn't matter how many are checked off—your fine is still twenty dollars." They laugh.

The tiny jail is not what I expected. A one-story cream building with blue trim houses all the inmates. Two doors separate the main road from the prison yard. And only five strands of barbwire atop a chain link fence dictate the boundaries of the criminals' freedom.

Inside the yard, dirty-looking laundry and bags of empty bottles are strung under a tin roof. Several male prisoners chop firewood with machetes. Others sit at a table. The missionaries approach them with warm greetings and hand out hymnals. Together they sing.

At the cross, at the cross, where I first saw the light,
And the burden of my heart rolled away,

It was there by faith I received my sight,
And now I am happy all the day!

Was it for crimes that I had done,
He groaned upon the tree?
Amazing pity! Grace unknown!
And love beyond degree!

One of the missionaries gives a short talk, and then the pastor stands up to address the men. The prisoners suddenly seem more alert and attentive.

The pastor's message focuses on the freedom available through Christ. "Remember," he says, "God loves and accepts each one of you just the way you are."

"Is that the end of the service?" I ask a missionary sitting nearby.

"Yeah, we only get a half hour. The Baptists have already been here, and the Catholics are coming next."

On the way out I see a large Yapese woman talking to an officer through the window at the first door. Her skin is dark and leathery; her blue dress equally worn.

"That was Justin's mom," one of the missionaries tells me after we leave. She's also spent time in jail for killing one of her sons when he was around five or six.

"She visits Justin now?" I ask.

"Yeah, for a long time no one could see him. Not even his family. They were keeping him in solitary confinement, but he was with the group today."

"He was?"

"Yeah, he's the guy I was talking to near the end. He asked who you were and what you were doing here. I told him you're writing a book about Kirsten."

"What did he say about that?"

"He said, 'Cool,' and told me he's thinking of writing a letter to her parents, or writing out his version of events and having it translated into English."

I'm not sure how I feel about Justin Ayin knowing my purpose so early on, but I hope it means he'll be willing to talk to me.

* * * * *

That afternoon the SMs take me to Ramung—otherwise known as the "forbidden island" on the northernmost tip of Yap. The home we're staying in for the weekend has one wall, a tin roof supported by wooden posts, and a bamboo/cement floor.

"It's rare that foreigners get to come here," Aila says. "You have to know someone and be invited."

Our group was invited by one of the student's parents, who offered to lend us their house. It's located in a mangrove swamp on the shore of the ocean. Two sides are bordered by water, which comes up the cement steps almost to the living level. Two sides are bordered by dry ground. I pick a spot in the ocean corner.

The entire night I'm harassed by wind, rain, and mosquitoes. I wake to find a crab pulling its shell across the floor in front of me. *So this is what it's like to live in nature,* I think as I grab my watch and glance at the time: 3:30 A.M. I look around. Ana and Sterling are asleep in hammocks. Everyone else is spread out on the floor. For several hours I read and swat mosquitoes. Then I notice Tyler stir in the center of the room. His eyes drift my direction.

"Good morning," I mouth. "Want to go for a walk?"

He nods, and we tiptoe around the sleepers to a grassy path our hosts led us down yesterday.

"Why don't we go the other direction?" I suggest. The path meanders along the beach, taking us by traditional meetinghouses and rows of stone money. We marvel at the beauty of the sunrise, the lush greenery, and the endless crab holes that make the ground soft and mushy. We're halfway back when we see one of our hosts coming toward us, yelling and waving her arms frantically.

"How far did you go?" she demands.

"To the bottom of the hill," I answer.

Her face scrunches, and when she speaks her voice sounds more angry than concerned. "You need to stay with the group," she says. "You could get in so much trouble. The villagers will be angry because you crossed the line. Didn't you see the line?"

I look at Tyler. Neither of us saw anything resembling a territory marker.

She continues reprimanding us until we reach the house, where I apologize once more and resume my spot in the corner. The woman calls after me.

"Don't go anywhere unless we all go together," she says. I nod in compliance and content myself watching crabs, lizards, and rats scurry around the mangroves.

By midmorning our Yapese hosts are ready to lead us around the island, but first they don our heads with braided leis and hand us each a cluster of leafy green branches.

"Why do we have to carry these?" Ana asks.

"They symbolize that you come in peace."

When we return to campus, I tell Lorraine about my experience.

"Oh, yes," she says. "Sometimes people carry a green leafy branch even when walking on the main road that runs by the school."

"*Hmm,*" I say, and I think about Kirsten.

* * * * *

The road where Kirsten was murdered is broad and paved. It winds up past the school, curving left and then right. The edges teem with greenery—waist-high grass, bushes with red flowers, coconut trees, and thick tangles of branches. A metal guardrail runs along most of one side. There are very few houses or connecting roads.

We drive back and forth several times until the missionaries find the spot.

"Up until last month this place was always covered in flowers," one of the guys says. "But just recently they cleared the area."

He parks on the side of the road, and we walk to the place.

"I think they found her body over there, where the ground starts sloping," he says, pointing to the tall grass between two coconut trees. I take a few steps, parting the grass with my hands. I notice what looks like hack marks on one of the trees. I recall one officer's account of the events. He said Justin confessed to knocking Kirsten over with his bike, then throwing her against a tree and holding her there with his hands—a story the officer thought plausible since he found the headlight she wore at the base of a tree.

Kirsten's autopsy report determined that Kirsten died of multiple stab wounds. Justin Ayin denied to police that he raped Kirsten but admitted touching her inappropriately. Justin later told someone that he didn't plan to kill Kirsten—but that she fought too hard.

The sun is burning hot overhead, and the guys sit down on the grass. Aila stands behind them. We linger near the area while the missionaries recount the day of the murder.

"It was the students who found her," Seth says, eyes cast downwards. "Afterward they went into shock. Some were shaking uncontrollably. Others went into fits of rage and started throwing furniture. I don't think they were ready to see that."

Aila looks up. "I don't think you're ever ready to see that."

CHAPTER 13

Be It Resolved

Four days later a Yapese senator, Jesse Raglmar, picks Tyler and me up from the school and takes us to the government office in the center of Colonia. When we arrive, Senator Falan is on the phone, drinking out of a mug with his picture on it and threatening to fund his own telecommunications company if the Internet and phone service on Yap does not improve.

"It will just be a minute," Senator Raglmar says, and provides us with some bananas to eat while we wait in the lobby.

Finishing his call, Senator Falan enthusiastically shakes our hands and leads us into the senate room.

"Where are you from?" he asks once we're seated.

"Michigan," I answer. "Though I attend the same university Kirsten is from in Tennessee."

"Michigan!" he says. "I went to school there!"

Both of the senators completed their college education in the States before serving in the Yapese government.

Senator Falan begins by expressing his sentiments regarding Kirsten's murder. "This illustrates a drastic change from when I was young," he says. "It used to be we gave preferential treatment to visitors and outsiders, treating them equal to or better than our own family members. This event is a blow to our sense of dignity and humanity—very un-islander!

"When I went to America, my sponsor there said, 'No one comes to my country and leaves with a negative impression.' That's why . . . " Senator Falan continues, tearing up, "it's so hard for me to accept a situation like this."

He wipes his eyes with a tissue. "Please forgive me for getting emotional. I was the one who invited the Adventist mission to come to Yap. Before living here I was in Pohnpei, and my daughter went to kindergarten at the Adventist school. By the time she was done with one year there, she could comprehend more English than I could when I graduated from elementary school. It was a very valuable and profound experience for my family.

"Once we came to Yap, I tried to enroll her in the private Catholic school, but it was full. So I wrote to the Adventist school in Palau and asked them to come establish a school here. Many people accused me of going against my Catholic religion or not supporting the public school system, but the Adventist school did so many good things for us. I offered them some land I own in Maap, but the location was too far away to be good. When we finally had a place, all my friends and family came out, and together we dug the foundation ditch for what is now the apartment building.

"Eventually Maranatha came in to build the rest, and it went up so fast! It was the big talk of the town at that time that even women came with Maranatha and were helping with the construction.

"The first year the school had about fifty students; the second year enrollment doubled. Many transferred from the public schools because there was such a good education being offered at the Adventist school. They have done so many good things for us, but had I anticipated this event with Kirsten would happen, I probably wouldn't have invited the Adventist school to come here."

"We were shocked in this small community," Senator Raglmar adds. "This is the first time an incident like this has occurred in this community, but we realize it's not the first in the world. That's why we want to memorialize this incident, to let people know there is zero tolerance in any community, not only for Kirsten, but for all victims of such heinous crimes. We can't control the incidents; we can only control our resolve for the future."

"Everything that we're doing now," Senator Falan says, "is to try to make our own existing after the event normal. You know? Kirsten doesn't benefit from this. All we're doing now is actually for us living. Senator Raglmar wrote a resolution that very day."

Senator Raglmar hands me a packet.

> Resolution No. 7-2021: Expressing a deep sense of loss and sorrow by members of the Seventh Legislature and the people of the State of Yap and conveying deep and sincere condolences to the parents, family members and friends of the late Kirsten Elisabeth Wolcott, a fine and promising young woman, whose tragic and untimely passing has shocked and devastated our community and bewildered our children, especially the students at Yap [Adventist] [s]chool who have lost a wonderful teacher and a wonderful friend.
>
> WHEREAS, at 5:30 a.m. each day without fail, Kirsten Elisabeth Wolcott, after she arranged all of her class teaching materials and papers in her room, took off on her early morning jog and she was never late to her class but on Thursday morning November 19, 2009 was different, she never came back to the school at the time she usually does; and
>
> WHEREAS, Miss Kirsten Elisabeth Wolcott was found a victim of a cowardly and cruel homicidal act of one sick individual, whose brutal and inhumane act has marred the atmosphere of our otherwise pristine and peaceful community in which Miss Kirsten had become a fine and

contributing member, and her tragic passing has shocked the people of the entire State of Yap, the Yap [Adventist] school and most especially the students, who loved their teacher and the parents, who loved their daughter and the many friends, who loved Kirsten and who are loved by her; and

WHEREAS, Miss Kirsten Elisabeth Wolcott who was only twenty years old was originally from Laneview, Virginia, in the United States and has been in Yap since school began in August, 2009 as a Seventh-day Adventist student missionary volunteer teacher at Yap [Adventist] [s]chool and had the reputation of being one of the best teachers at [Adventist], who was not only loved by her students but also by the teachers at the school; and

WHEREAS, Miss Wolcott had taken the year off from Southern Adventist University in Collegedale, Tennessee, where she was a junior education major, and after a year of teaching at Yap [Adventist] [s]chool she was to return to complete the requirements for her degree and graduate with a BA in Education; and

WHEREAS, the people of the State of Yap are full of sadness and sorrow for the tragic and untimely passing of Miss Kirsten Elisabeth Wolcott, a fine and promising young woman who was ready to achieve her dream of a more enlightened and tolerant world, and during this dark and sad hour, the hearts of the entire people of Yap goes out to Dr. and Mrs. Wolcott and Kirsten's brothers and all members of the Wolcott family and friends of Kirsten; and

WHEREAS, the Seventh Legislature of the State of Yap vehemently condemns these cruel and cowardly acts against humanity by individuals, who have lost their own humanity; and

WHEREAS, the Seventh Legislature of the State of Yap joins the Governor and the leaders of Yap State and the head of every household in the state in declaring our vehement condemnation of this act and our resolve to undertake swift and effective measures to bring the perpetrator under custody and to justice, and to ensure that such violent and cruel act do not occur again in the State of Yap; and now, therefore,

BE IT RESOLVED by the Seventh Legislature of the State of Yap, Third Regular Session, 2009, that the Legislature hereby expresses a deep sense of loss and sorrow by the members of the Seventh Legislature and the people of the State of Yap and convey deep and sincere condolences to the parents, family members and friends of the late Kirsten Wolcott, a fine and promising young woman, whose tragic and untimely passing has shocked and devastated our community, robbed us of her achievements, and bewildered our children, especially the student at Yap [Adventist] [s]chool who have lost a wonderful teacher and a wonderful friend; and

BE IT FURTHER RESOLVED, that this Day, Thursday, November 19, be remembered and observed each year as the Memorial Day in remembrance of Kirsten Elisabeth Wolcott and all innocent victims of violent crimes against humanity in the State of Yap and in the world today; and

BE IT FURTHER RESOLVED, that a permanent memorial be erected at the site of the incident and the portion of the road from the Tagreng Bridge to Short Stop Store be named Kirsten Elisabeth Wolcott Memorial Road; and

BE IT FURTHER RESOLVED, that the copies of this Resolution be transmitted to Mr. and Mrs. Wolcott, the

President of the Guam-Micronesia Mission of the Seventh-day Adventist Church, the Principal and faculty of Yap Seventh-day Adventist School, U.S. Ambassador to the Federated States of Micronesia, President of the Federated States of Micronesia, Speaker of the Congress of the Federated States of Micronesia, Governor of the State of Yap, Members of the Executive Cabinet, all heads of programs and agencies and offices, all village, municipal and island leaders in the State of Yap, Chairman and members of the Council of Pilung and Chairman of the council of Tamol.

* * * * *

"In the Yapese culture, people don't want to talk about death," Senator Falan says. "Out of respect for the deceased and their surviving family members, they don't even mention the name again. As a result, many times I have been labeled as a radical for taking a proactive approach in calling attention to the incident."

"But we have gone out and seen things done differently in other places and cultures," Senator Raglmar says. "We need to look at the situation through a different pair of eyes, not as an offense, but as a lesson. The purpose of the resolution is to create memorials in areas she emphasized as important, like education. In addition to this, we organized a drive to establish a scholarship foundation in her name. In the future, there might even be scholarships for teachers. The Chamber of Commerce and the business community are providing the money.

"The passing of the resolution was unique in itself because it called public attention to the event and let them know we need to do something. It alerted other responsible authorities in the community that times have changed."

"Christian values," Senator Falan adds, "used to be here even before Christians. They survived through changing governments and situations."

"You could leave a basket here for one week and it would still be here. No one would touch it," Senator Raglmar says.

"But these days," Senator Falan says, "I'm hearing more 'I,' 'me,' and less 'we,' 'us.' "

"What do you think caused the change?" I ask.

"Modernization," Senator Raglmar answers. "We are developed now."

"But Kirsten's contribution to us is strengthening our values," Senator Falan says. "We have to remember that while other parts of our society change, the core elements cannot: how we care and how we value other people. But never mind all of this. What can we do for you?"

"Everything you've shared so far is very interesting," I tell them. Then I make my requests. My third is a chance to speak with Justin Ayin. The senators glance at one another.

"As far as the first two requests," Senator Raglmar says, "We're happy to help you. But to see Ayin . . ."

"As far as me, I have no desire to see him!" Senator Falan says, waving his hands. "I hate to have anything to do with that kind of people!" His voice rises in pitch. "That's not Yapese! That's not how we do things!"

"It will be very difficult," Senator Raglmar says. "The case is still in progress, so we would have to speak with his attorney as well as the Attorney General. You know, usually you would wait to do the interviews until the case is done and everything has come out, but I guess since the timing of your book, that's why you want to do it now. Anyway, we'll check on it, but I can't guarantee anything."

"I understand," I say. "Thank you for being willing to attempt."

As our visit draws to a close, Senator Falan reaches under the table and pulls out a heavy necklace made with green, orange, and brown stones. The pendant on the bottom is a four-inch whale tooth.

"This is a traditional necklace worn by very special guests on special occasions," he says. "We consider the purpose of your visit to our island very special, and so we would like to honor you by giving you this. Please wear it while you are here conducting research for your book."

"And please, let us know anything we can do for you," Senator Raglmar adds. "We are very happy to help. Miss Wolcott was an amazing young woman."

CHAPTER 14

The Interview

The following Tuesday, Tyler and I pedal into town using Kirsten's and Liz's old bikes. Over the past few months, they've broken down. Kirsten's is missing brakes, and Liz's a pedal.

"Whew! How did Kirsten make it up these hills?" I ask Tyler. "I'm starting to have a lot of sympathy for Liz. I don't think it was just that peach nectar."

Exhausted, we arrive at the government building. Senator Raglmar gives us a warm welcome when we walk in.

"I've talked to Justin's attorney," he tells me. "And he's very uncomfortable with the idea of you interviewing Justin. As you know, it's more customary for you to do this sort of thing after the case is closed."

I nod in understanding and ask if it would be possible for me to speak with Justin's attorney. Senator Raglmar says Yes, and gives me directions to the attorney's office around the corner.

* * * * *

Tyler and I are sweaty and splattered in mud. Not a great first impression, I think, as I try to tidy my appearance.

We push open a wooden door and enter a cramped office. I

greet the woman at the front desk and ask to speak with the defense attorney. A wiry man emerges from behind a wooden partition and introduces himself as Joe Dalman, Justin's public defender. We follow him behind the partition, stepping over stacks of papers and eventually finding a seat on metal folding chairs.

I introduce myself and my purpose—and then ask for permission to speak with Justin.

"I don't know," he says. He's hesitant since Justin has not yet been charged for crimes related to Kirsten's murder.

In 2008, Justin was charged with unlawful possession of marijuana, burglary, and assault and battery. The court put him on probation until 2014 on the basis that he would not violate any penal law. At the time of Kirsten's murder, Justin was still on probation for these three charges.

The day of Kirsten's murder, Justin was arrested on suspicion, taken to the police office, and questioned. He escaped while the officers were taking him to the fire station next door to be weighed. Three and a half hours later, he was recaptured, and shackles were put around his ankles. Prosecution resumed on his former charges, and two new charges were added: escape and violation of probation.

In February 2010, Justin pled guilty to these two charges. He was sentenced to imprisonment until 2016. As part of the plea agreement, the unlawful possession of marijuana and the assault and battery charges were dismissed.

According to Attorney General Victor Nabeyan, Justin has twice confessed to murdering Kirsten: once in a recorded confession and once in a signed statement. The court has not yet charged him because they are waiting for evidence from the FBI.

* * * * *

Mr. Dalman says that he'll let me conduct the interview if Justin agrees.

"Call me on Wednesday around three o'clock, and I'll let you know what Justin says," Mr. Dalman says.

On Wednesday I call back.

"Justin has agreed to speak with you, so meet me at my office on Friday at one o'clock. Then we'll go over together."

On Friday I walk over to the jail with Mr. Dalman, and we wait on a bench while an officer goes to get Justin. I've heard many things about Justin prior to this visit, and I'm not sure what to expect.

"He's weak and lamblike," one person told me. "His shoulders are hunched over, and his eyes are always downcast. He talks so softly you can barely hear him."

A set of chained feet enter through the doorway. I look up and see Justin, appearing neither weak nor lamblike. He has a shaved head and square jaw with a black goatee. A cut-off T-shirt reveals dark, muscular arms.

"Hi, I'm Rainey. Thank you for agreeing to speak with me."

He nods.

We move into a small room, and Justin takes a seat across from me. His defense attorney offers him some betel nut, a native fruit that the Yapese chew as a mild stimulant. Justin takes it eagerly. I watch as he peels away the green layer. Long fingernails curl from his left hand.

"He hasn't cut them since the day of the murder," someone told me. "He says it's a reminder."

I ask Justin to confirm.

"I may have a reason for keeping them long. I may not," he says.

We move on.

Dark, knit eyebrows give his face a hard expression, but underneath, alert eyes show flashes of emotion: worry, fear—regret?

He speaks some English, but not well, so his defense attorney translates.

"He wants to express his inner feelings about what happened in relationship to Kirsten," he says.

I nod and lean forward, ready.

* * * * *

For twenty minutes, Justin shares with me his background. He's twenty-six and married. He grew up on Yap in the village of Gagil—a short distance past Tom's Store. For a while he attended the Adventist school, but left in eighth grade after being caught smoking cigarettes.

"They told me to eat soap, so I don't want to eat soap," he says. Instead, he left. Around the same time, he got in trouble with the authorities for throwing rocks at a school bus and was sentenced to three months in prison.

"And you were eleven years old?" I ask. "How did you feel when you went to prison?"

"I feel bad, because that's the first time," he says.

The discussion segues into his most recent crime.

"What motivated you to kill Kirsten?" I ask.

"You're not allowed to ask that," Mr. Dalman says.

"How do you feel after the fact—now?"

"Sad," Justin answers. "Of course, uh, I feel bad. Feel sad."

"Were you under the influence of drugs, or were you drunk at the time?"

"Both."

"What drugs?"

"Marijuana."

"Where were you coming from?"

"Gagil. At a friend's house."

"Were you walking, or on a bike?" I ask.

His attorney interrupts. "You cannot ask that question."

I nod and move on, but the attorney blocks each of my succeeding questions.

"We're not talking about the incident," he says, "because it might conflict with the statement he gave to the police."

"Can I ask, had you seen Kirsten before?"

Justin seems confused by this question. He tells me he's been at the school since they built the apartment building. I try again.

"When was the first time that you saw Kirsten?"

Mr. Dalman translates my question and then Justin's answer. "He said the first time, uh . . . he saw her is the, uh . . . that's the time of the incident.

"The only thing," Mr. Dalman says, "he can relate to regarding Kirsten is uh, . . . he heard about her being, uh . . . Adventist teacher and jogging every morning and evening in the road . . . from some other . . . uh, friends."

"I've heard that at the time of your capture you had items that you'd been taking from the apartment at the school. Is that true?"

"Yeah, it is."

"That's true?"

"Yeah, that's true."

He and the attorney exchange a few more words in Yapese. Sensing some confusion, I ask, "You took them this year?"

"No," his attorney says. "That was before."

"When before?"

Justin answers. "Maybe three years."

"Three years ago? Were there girls in the apartment when you went in?"

"There is," Justin says.

"Can you tell me about that incident?"

He and the attorney speak in Yapese for a minute.

"There were people," his attorney says.

"And what was your intention?" I ask.

Justin answers, "Yeah, to take some items, like uh, take a cell phone."

"Did you harass any of the girls?"

"Yeah."

"How many?"

He and the attorney speak in Yapese. Mr. Dalman translates. "She put her, uh—" Justin interrupts, making a shoving motion with his arm.

The attorney continues. "He went to pick up the telephone and one lady woke up and he pushed her down and then he ran away."

"So it was in the night?"

"Yeah, yes, it was," Justin says.

I continue to ask questions, but each of them is blocked. I can tell the attorney is growing impatient. I decide to close the interview with one further offer.

"Is there anything else you might like to share or add?" I ask.

Justin spends a long time talking to the attorney in Yapese.

"Somehow," his attorney translates, "if things can be back to where it was, knowing that, uh . . . Kirsten is a very good person, he'd like to express sorrow for what happened to the parents. He doesn't know her, but he heard so much about her, especially after the incident. You know people here in Yap were shocked such a thing had happened to a young, very nice person that came to help the people here in Yap. That's something that bothers him all the time."

"What will happen with Justin now?" I ask the attorney as we walk back to his office.

"Now we will work to get a reduced sentence," he says. "There are many people on Yap who would like to kill him. Right now jail is the safest place."

* * * * *

Eleven days later, Justin wrote a letter and sent it to the Wolcotts.

Greeting and salutation from Yap Island, and in particular, Justin A.

This the first time that I am writing after a long time of
soul searching, meditation, kind prayer. I have come to
the point where I feel confident enough to write to you,
kind, humbly, ask for your forgiveness. I know that I
don't deserve any, but I have to ask now that I have the
opportunity. I hope and pray that by now Pastor Rojas
will have delivered my verbal message of apology to you
all.

June 1, 2010—Morning, Tuesday
Justin A.

CHAPTER 15

A Time for Everything

Back at the school it's business as usual. The guys are chopping coconuts, and the girls are writing lesson plans. One of the dogs is lying at the foot of the steps, hoping to get a head scratch or a scrap of food.

"I can't believe you're leaving tomorrow," one of the missionaries says. "It feels more like you're one of us now than that you're here to gather information for a book."

I smile, knowing what she means.

"Don't write that I'm bad at volleyball," Sterling had joked earlier in the week. I told him that I just might.

I've felt a deepening bond with this group.

"So are you happy with how the trip went and all the information you got?" Gus asks.

"Yeah, I am. I couldn't have asked for a better trip."

* * * * *

That evening I knock on the Fonsekas door. I want to say Goodbye and thank them for their hospitality, since my plane is leaving early in the morning.

Miss Mary answers and invites me inside. I take a seat on the couch and watch as Mr. Fonseka pours me a glass of cold orange juice. I haven't spent much time with them during the last two weeks, but as I look at them now, I see faces worn with tiredness and grief.

Principal Fonseka leans on the kitchen table and stares out the window after handing me the glass. "So many times I ask myself, 'Why did she go out running in the dark?' I knew she sometimes ran on the road during daylight, but I never knew she went in the dark. If I had, I would have put a stop to it."

Miss Mary is sitting across from me on another couch, trying hard to hold back tears. "Kirsten was like a daughter to me," she says. "I don't know why, but since the beginning I felt like I connected with her most out of the group. We were supposed to cook together that weekend, but we never got to."

For a half hour the Fonsekas reminisce about what they could have done differently to prevent the situation, but none of the options seem to bring peace. When I'd spoken with Principal Fonseka a few days earlier, he described the confusion about what Kirsten was allowed to do. "I tried to look for the permission letter Kirsten gave me from her parents," he said. "But I could never find it. Now her parents tell me it said she could only bike off campus, but to me at the time I thought, *Biking, exercising—whatever. It's the same thing.*"

"Where do you plan to go now?" I ask them, knowing they've already stayed longer than their volunteer contract requires.

"At the beginning of this year, we were planning to leave," Mr. Fonseka says. "But now we've decided to stay another year."

"I hope we get a good group of missionaries," Miss Mary adds. "This year we had such a good group—I can't understand why this happened."

Tears stream down her face. "But I keep trying to trust God. Somehow He will work this together, right?"

* * * * *

That evening I walk out to the deck. The sun is setting—the glorious pink and orange I've come to expect. As I look across the campus where Kirsten once jogged, I think about how her life was so abruptly cut short.

"Why didn't God answer her prayers?" I've heard some ask. "She prayed every day for safety before she went running."

It's true—she did. But I think about something Kirsten wrote the month before she arrived in Yap.

Solomon says there is a time for everything, Kirsten journaled after reading Ecclesiastes 3:1–8. *As I studied I wondered why there are both bad and good things. Why should there be a time for death? I wondered if it was to bring us closer to God. But then as I read the commentary I realized that it was to illustrate that nothing lasts forever. There is a time for good and it may last awhile, but then it will always go away and bad will come. Life is always changing so we shouldn't sit around being idle, waiting for the good stuff to happen. We never know when our "time" is, and so we should take every advantage of the good times we have and work hard to get through the bad times with the help of Jesus Christ because He wants to help us . . .*

Think about it: someone dies every second. Do you think that many of them expected to die? I want my heart to be prepared for death. I want my life to be lived so that there is something good to say about me when I'm gone, and hopefully my death can lead others to eternal life! Come fill my heart today with Your thoughts, words, and actions so that I can be a "silent" witness with my actions. God, help me to live each moment like it was my last so that I will be ready when my time actually comes.

Love Ya. Amen.

Afterword
by Hollis Wolcott

Kirsten's dad, Hollis, wrote the following tribute for her funeral service, which took place on November 29, 2009.

My precious Kirsten,

I want to thank you for all the wonderful years you gave me the opportunity to be your father. What a joy and a wonder it was to watch you grow and mature. I was always your favorite love until another Man stole your heart, but I was overjoyed at that also because He was tall and gentle and had the kindest eyes and His name was Jesus. You spent lots of time each day reading His love letters and talking with Him and writing letters back. Your relationship grew and grew and it was wonderful to watch.

I want to thank you for all the wonderful music that you played for me: the music from the piano chimes, your harp, and your voice. I have not yet told Isabella, your harp, of the news, but I am sure she heard as many kind friends came and went yesterday and we prayed and cried together and shared memories of you.

I want to thank you for the many friends that you made in our community by singing in community choirs, teaching in daycare, leading our last Vacation Bible School, teaching Sabbath School, helping at community service and sometimes assisting me in a night emergency at the office helping someone in pain. Many from the community today called and wrote to send their love and memories.

I thank you for the walks we took together through our woods. They are beautiful today with the sun shining on the beautiful golden autumn leaves. You can see the river clearly from the overlook point and it is beautiful. I remember that is where you always wanted me to build your house when you got married. I will build that house in my imagination for you and you will live there and I will visit you and your husband often. It will only be a temporary home because the real home you wanted to build is the one in heaven that our Lord promised you could build. I know you wanted to build the rooms with vines that had flowers, since you loved flowers so very much.

I want to thank you for Sandy, your dog that you loved so much. I remember the day you and I stopped at a house with a handwritten sign that said "Puppies—free to a good home," and picked out that little ball of whimpering fur. I remember how you held her so carefully in your lap all the way home. I remember calling your mom and telling her we had a new family member. Yesterday when each loving guest came to our home, Sandy barked as usual, but she seemed to know something was wrong because every time I petted her she whined and softly cried. I will take wonderful care of Sandy for you, I promise.

I want to thank you for giving your mother and me twenty wonderful years. Most know you by Kirsten but you will always be my little "Peeper"—my special name for you. To others of your friends you were "Keke." I do not know what special name Jesus has for you, but I do know He has one and I look forward to that day when I will find out what it is. I want to remind you that the best-made harps and the best harp teachers are waiting for you soon. The animals you loved will all be so beautiful and friendly, and the flowers will be even prettier than the beautiful pictures you sent of the flowers on Yap. Best of all, we will reserve a special banquet room and invite all the people whose lives you touched and we will invite as Guest of honor, Jesus Himself. Oh Peeper, what a wonderful meeting that will be. The stories everyone will tell will be simply wonderful. You will play your golden harp for special music, and again I will be so proud of you. Jesus will thank you for your special music and call you by your special name that I do not yet know. Then He will stand and spread His arms in blessing to us all and we will see the nail scars, but He will read our minds and assure us that the pain was nothing compared to the friends before Him. He will assure us all that we will be with Him and the Father and the Holy Spirit forever where there is no more pain or sorrow or crying. So Peeper, goodbye for now till I see you again very soon.

With all my love,
Pap

Acknowledgments

Like all projects, this one would not have been possible without the encouragement and support of many people. I'm particularly grateful to:

The Wolcotts—For entrusting me with their family's story and generously allowing me to become a part of their lives.

Dr. Andy Nash—For your invaluable insight and encouragement. Thank you for guiding me through each step of the writing process, from inspiration to publication.

Vanessa Cutz—For willingly accompanying me on the trip to Virginia.

Tyler Barrows—For believing in this project enough to assist me with my research in Yap. Thank you for being a selfless travel partner—willing to sleep in huts with crabs, eat peanut butter and bread for two weeks, and bike downhill without brakes.

My mom, Deborah—For praying me through everything, believing in me always, and supporting me in every possible way.

My sister, Kimberly—For patiently listening to draft after draft and pushing me to write more descriptively.

Sari Butler—For knowing I would be a writer before I did, and leaving voicemails all summer that said, "Write five pages, then call me back!"

Chris Clouzet—For being a willing soundboard and sharing my enthusiasm over this project.

My journalism professors and friends—For chipping in whenever I needed help writing a letter, coming up with a transitional verb, or choosing between two sentences.

The Yapese Legislature and Authorities—For their enthusiastic cooperation and support.

Financial supporters—For making my trip to Yap and the telling of this story possible through generous donations.

And to the many people who shared their memories of Kirsten with me.

Photos

Kirsten's family. *From left to right:* brother Scott, dad Hollis, Kirsten, brother Nathan, and mom Karen.

Kirsten and her mom at Southern's mother-daughter banquet, held during her freshman year of college.

Kirsten's second-grade class on the playground at recess.

The balcony with the door to Kirsten's apartment.

The missionaries enjoy a Friday night dinner on the balcony. *From left to right:* Olivia, Sterling, Alex, Seth, Kirsten, and Liz.

Kirsten, Liz, and Alex lead song service at a local village, where the missionaries frequently went on Sabbath to spend time with the children.

Scott, Sterling, and Alex lead song service for children in a local village.

The five girls who shared an apartment smile for a picture on one of Yap's beaches. *From left to right:* Aila, Kirsten, Katherine, Olivia, and Liz.

Kirsten and her roommate Katherine snorkel in the Pacific Ocean.

The road where Kirsten was murdered (though the specific location is not shown in this picture). Alex, Ana, Aila, and the black puppy walk back to the school.

Justin Ayin answering questions during my interview with him.

The view from Kirsten's balcony in Yap.

Seth, Kirsten, and Liz stand on the edge of campus that overlooks an ocean inlet.

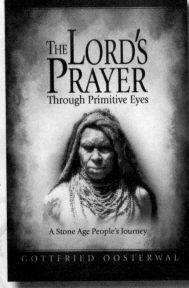